HOW COLLABORATIVE LEADERS CONSTRUCT POWER: EXPLORING A NEW LEADERSHIP DISCOURSE

A dissertation submitted by

VALERIE J. DAVIS, MSOD, MA

to

FIELDING GRADUATE UNIVERSITY

in partial fulfillment of the requirements for the degree of

DOCTOR OF PHILOSOPHY

in

HUMAN DEVELOPMENT

This dissertation has been accepted for the faculty of Fielding Graduate University by

Katrina S. Rogers, PhD, Chair

Committee Members:
Judith Stevens-Long, PhD, Faculty Reader
Tojo Thatchenkery, PhD, Faculty Reader
Declan Fitzsimons, PhD, External Examiner
Ana M. Barrio, PhD, Student Reader

ProQuest Number: 10160008

All rights reserved

INFORMATION TO ALL USERS
The quality of this reproduction is dependent upon
the quality of the copy submitted.

In the unlikely event that the author did not send a complete
manuscript and there are missing pages, these will be noted. Also,
if material had to be removed, a note will indicate the deletion.

ProQuest 10160008

Published by ProQuest LLC (2016).
Copyright of the Dissertation is held by the Author.

All rights reserved.
This work is protected against unauthorized copying under Title 17,
United States Code Microform Edition © ProQuest LLC.

ProQuest LLC.
789 East Eisenhower Parkway
P.O. Box 1346
Ann Arbor, MI 48106 - 1346

How Collaborative Leaders Construct Power: Exploring a New Leadership Discourse

by

Valerie J. Davis

Abstract

This study explores how leaders who are identified as collaborative construct power. Power is a concept fundamental to leadership and yet is an area that is not well studied in the literature that investigates collaborative approaches. While this is principally a study of individual leaders' thoughts about power, it also considers how leaders sustain their constructions through systems and structures, and how power manifests in their relationship with followers. The findings indicate that collaborative leaders construct power in broader terms than is typical of the leadership literature. They view power as a neutral social force that can be expressed in multiple ways, inclusive of, but not limited to the act of dominating others. They show a preference for mutualistic expressions of power and construct systems and structures in support of that preference. When viewed from a relationship dynamics perspective, mutualistic power between leaders and followers is enabled by their promotion of relational equality. Additional findings indicate that the leaders in this study view power as a capacity that can be learned, and that followers hold the potential for that capacity. They do not believe that power is a possession to be given to another, as in empowerment. Rather, they view the leader's role to be one of accompaniment and of creating the conditions to encourage and support capacity development.

Key words: collaborative leadership, power, constructivism, social construction, entitative, relational, qualitative, multimethodological.

Copyright by

VALERIE JEAN DAVIS

2016

ACKNOWLEDGEMENTS

A dear friend warned me at the onset of my PhD journey that it could be a lonely one. In so many ways she was right. There are many long hours spent reading, writing, and reflecting. But for me these hours were balanced with equally long and fruitful times engaging with numerous people who encouraged me to push forward. I am truly grateful for having received the wisdom and support of many wonderful people.

To begin, I want to thank my Committee. Katrina Rogers, you have walked with me almost from day one and kept me going when I thought I could not. You are an amazing woman and I have been so lucky to have you as my mentor and chair. Thank you for the innumerable contributions you have made to my growth as a scholar. Judith Stevens-Long has worked with me almost as long. As a subject matter expert in adult development and a writing expert, you motivated me to aspire to greater standards, guided me to focus my thoughts and to express them more eloquently. I am so happy that you were able to work with me right to the finish. Tojo Thatchenkary stepped in late to the Committee and more than made up for this in all of his brilliant contributions. Thank you Tojo for your candour and compliments. You are a true scholar. Ana Barrio went well beyond the role of student reader. Thank you for working with me throughout my entire journey, for the monthly calls, and the extensive feedback. You are the best. Declan Fitzsimons took his role as external examiner to heart and spent endless hours providing me with thoughtful and well crafted feedback. Thank you all for giving so much of yourselves. Finally, I would be remiss if I did not mention Gayla Napier, my *shadow* student reader. Gayla was the third party on those monthly calls and has been a true friend and colleague since my first day at Fielding.

There are some other people who inspired and motivated me on this journey. I want to thank Haleh Arbab and Caren Rosenthal for allowing me to participate in the pilot program *Constructing a Conceptual Framework for Social Action*. It was during that week that I decided to apply for this program. And thank you for asking me to work with you to launch the online program. The experience of collaborating with the group of volunteers you assembled was truly life changing. I also want to thank Beth Bowen, Arthur Dahl, John Hatcher, and Debbie Monroe for providing me with recommendations. I hold a special place in my heart for each of you. Thank you to Wes Gee and Daniel Truran who helped me find my participants. There would be no study without you. And a special thank you to Daniel for the many other roles he played along the way in providing me with invaluable assistance.

There are a group of people who also helped me to learn about the true spirit of collaboration. To all the members of the Local Assembly that I had the pleasure of working with over the years, thank you for being such incredible teachers: Bahiyyih Ancheta, Tara Ancheta, David Cooper, Michael Davids, Tyrone Davids, Beverley Davis, Vida Faridi, Mehry Kianfar, Arian Nejati, Ellie Nejati, Kamran Nejati, Mitra Nejati, Manouchehr Fanaeian, Faran Vafaie, Melanie Vafaie, Imran Vanat, Saifu Vanat, Paul Yates, and Vickie Yazdani.

Thank you to my loving family for your patience, support, encouragement, and cheerleading. There are two very special people that I have saved for last. Maureen O'Connor has read all of my work including endless drafts of this dissertation.

She always offered me sage advice. Thank you so much for everything. You are a true friend. Finally, to the most amazing woman in my life, my Mother, thank you will never be enough. I am so very glad that you are here to celebrate with me.

DEDICATION

To my loving parents,

Norman and Ursula

Words will never be enough to express my love and gratitude.

Thank you for always being there.

TABLE OF CONTENTS

CHAPTER ONE: INTRODUCTION 1
    Purpose 5
    Research Question 5
    Inspiration 5
    Definition of Terms 6
        Collaborative Leadership 6
        Power 7
        Construct 8
    Conceptual Framework 8
        Collaborative Leadership 9
        Power 10
        Agency and Communion 10
        Constructivism 11
    Methodology Overview 12
    Assumptions 13
    Significance 15
    Summary 16

CHAPTER TWO: REVIEW OF THE LITERATURE 18
    Collaborative Leadership Theories 20
        Origins 20
        Entitative and Relational Lenses 23
        Collaborative Leadership Theories 24
            Shared leadership 24
            Collective leadership 26
            Distributed leadership 27

- Relational Leadership. 28
- A Dialogue Among Entitative and Relational Theories 30
- Critique of Collaborative Leadership Theories 31
- Power 32
  - How Power is Constituted 32
    - Locutions of Power 34
  - Power as Capacity 37
  - Power as Capacity 38
  - Relational Power 39
  - Power and Leadership 42
  - Power and Structure 42
  - Power and Influence 44
- Agency and Communion 44
- Constructivism 48
  - Cognitive Theory 48
  - Social Constructionist Theory 49
  - Entitative and Relational Lenses 51
- Leadership and Power 52
- Summary 59
- Research Question 62
- CHAPTER THREE: METHODOLOGY 63
  - Epistemological Framework 64
  - Theoretical Perspective 66
    - Postpositivism 66
    - Interpretivism 67
  - Methodology 68
    - Phenomenology 68
    - Ethnography 69
  - Methods 70
    - Population Sampling 71

- Sample Size ... 72
- Recruitment Process ... 73
- Data Collection ... 75
  - Semistructured interviews ... 75
  - Group observations ... 76
  - Systems and structures ... 77
- Data Analysis ... 78
  - Semistructured interviews ... 78
  - Group observation ... 79
  - Systems and structures ... 80
- Synthesis ... 81
- Pilot Study ... 82
- Protection of Human Participants ... 83
- Trustworthiness of Study Findings ... 84
- Summary ... 86
- CHAPTER FOUR: KEY FINDINGS ... 87
- Study Participants ... 88
- Key Findings ... 92
  - Theme 1: Reflecting on Power ... 95
    - Power is a neutral force ... 96
    - Constructions of power are learned ... 97
  - Theme 2: Using Power ... 99
    - Inspiring ... 100
    - Releasing capacity ... 102
    - Role modeling ... 104
  - Theme 3: Abusing Power ... 106
    - Using power against ... 107
    - Gender issues ... 111
  - Theme 4: Relational Equality ... 113
    - Shared leadership ... 114

- Participatory decision-making. 114
- Respect for others 114
- Transparency in communication 115
- Theme 5: Innovating Strategic Frameworks 116
  - Overview 117
  - Principle-centered. 118
  - Values-based 120
  - Founded on collaboration. 121
  - Devolved leadership 122
  - Doing social good 123
- Theme 6: Shaping the Environment 123
- Leadership practices 124
  - Consulting others 125
  - Participatory decision-making 128
  - Working through conflict 129
  - Putting others ahead of self 131
  - Promoting relational equality 132
  - Valuing diversity 134
  - Transparency in communication. 136
- Character 138
  - Humility 139
  - Trustworthiness and trust 141
  - Courage 144
- Culture 147
  - Creates a supportive culture 147
  - Develops a learning organization 149
- Contradictory Findings 151
- Summary of Key Findings 157
- **CHAPTER FIVE: DISCUSSION** 160
  - Theme 1: Reflecting on Power 162

Theme 2: Using Power 165
Theme 3: Abusing Power 170
Summary 175
Theme 4: Relational Equality 176
Theme 5: Innovating Strategic Frameworks 180
Theme 6: Shaping the Environment 184
Additional Findings 188
Hierarchy and heterarchy 188
Balancing agency and communion. 190
Multicultural experiences 190
Summary 191
Implications for Scholarship 195
Implications for Practice 197
Recommendations for Future Research 198
Limitations of the Study 200
Concluding Remarks 201
References 203
Footnotes 229

LIST OF FIGURES

Figure 1. Conceptual Framework for the study 8
Figure 2. Duck/rabbit optical illusion. 15
Figure 3. A unified framework of power 38
Figure 4. Relational and distributive dimensions of power 41
Figure 5. Dialogue: four phases of learning conversations 60
Figure 6. Research question, emergent themes, and key findings. 161
Figure 7. Gender difference in the abuse of power. 174
Figure 8. Constellation of leadership practices. 185
Figure 9. Integral model of mutualistic power. 194

LIST OF TABLES

Table 1. Summary of Study Participants' Background Information 89
Table 2. Themes and Subthemes 93
Table 3. Theme 1: Reflecting on Power 96
Table 4. Theme 2: Using Power 100
Table 5. Theme 3: Abusing Power 107
Table 6. Theme 4: Relational Equality 113
Table 7. Theme 5: Innovating Strategic Frameworks 116
Table 8. Common Core Values 120
Table 9. Theme 6: Shaping the Environment 124
Table 10. Subtheme 1: Leadership Practices 126
Table 11. Subtheme 2: Character 139
Table 12. Subtheme 3: Culture 148

APPENDICES

Appendix A: Introductory Letter to Potential Participants 235

Appendix B: Interview Protocol 238

Appendix C: Organizational Documents Reviewed 243

Appendix D: Informed Consent.. 244

Appendix E: Study Participants 249

Appendix F: Values-based Capacity Development Framework 251

Appendix G: Governance Model Guiding Principles........................... 252

Appendix H: Cooperative identity, values & principles 254

Appendix I: Competencies of the Leadership Mastery Program 257

CHAPTER ONE

INTRODUCTION

The human race is being urged by the requirements of its own maturation to free itself from its inherited understanding and use of power. That it can do so is demonstrated by the fact that, although dominated by the traditional conception, humanity has always been able to conceive of power in other forms critical to its hopes. (Bahá'í International Community, 1995, p. 23)

This is a study of leadership. While it is widely recognized that the leadership literature is already vast (Bass & Bass, 2008; Hernandez, Eberly, Avolio, & Johnson, 2011; Yammarino, Salas, Serban, Shirreffs, & Shuffler, 2012; Yukl, 2013), there is an ongoing need to advance research. The concept of leadership has been defined and redefined many times (Bass & Bass, 2008; Northouse, 2010; Yukl, 2013). Despite this, Western cultures have largely endorsed command and control, directive, and hierarchical approaches where power is held by the few.

While such approaches may have served us in the past, rising numbers of indicators bring into question their continued usefulness and ability to meet current needs (Bradford & Cohen, 1998; Fletcher, 2004; Kellerman, 2012).

One such indicator is the recent barrage of organizational scandals. Names such as Bear Sterns, Enron, FIFA, Lehman Brothers, Volkswagen, and Worldcom are a few organizations among the increasing number that have become known for their leadership transgressions or failures. Another indicator is the rising number of challenges facing humanity. Over 50 years ago, Emery and Trist (1965) observed that our social worlds were becoming increasingly more complex. The concept of complexity derives from systems theory where the many parts of phenomena are understood to interact with each other in multiple ways. In the intervening period, since Emery and Trist made their observation, humanity has created progressively more complex social worlds, catalyzed in large part by technological advancements and the globalization of markets (Bass & Bass, 2008; Bennis, 1999; Schein, 2012; Uhl-Bien & Ospina, 2012). A host of seemingly intractable problems has resulted. The most prominent among these are climate change, escalating economic disparities, rising terrorism, massive population displacement, and the continuing threat of nuclear war. There are no immediate signs of these problems being resolved, or of the rise in complexity abating.

Deterring organizational scandals, rising above the heightening complexity, and resolving the growing numbers of complex problems requires leadership. However, leadership as it has traditionally been practiced has demonstrated that it is not up to the task. New approaches are needed to guide the generation of innovative approaches and solutions. In response to this need, increasing numbers of scholars are exploring leadership that emphasizes collaboration between leaders and followers.

Beginning in the early 1990s (Manz & Sims, 1991; Rost, 1993) and gaining momentum around the turn of the new millennium, a dialogue began in the literature about the need to explore more collaborative approaches to leadership as compared to the traditional, top-down, hierarchical approaches. Many contributors to this ongoing discourse stressed the need for leadership that better reflects our present-day world (Crevani, Lindgren, & Packendorff, 2007; Edmondson, 2012; Kramer & Crespy, 2011; Pearce & Conger, 2003; Raelin, 2011; Uhl-Bien, Marion, & McKelvey, 2007; Wegge, Jeppesen, & Weber, 2012). The approaches they explored are also thought to hold the possibility of counteracting "the wide-spread disappointment in and distrust of leaders in the society at large" (Kellerman, 2012, p. 169). Characteristic of these contemporary theories of leadership is the suggestion of a more equitable distribution of power between leaders and followers.

While the discourse in the leadership literature may be relatively recent, collaborative approaches are not (Bolden, 2011; Spillane & Sherer, 2004; Thorpe, Gold, & Lawler, 2011). However, inquiries into this approach have been overshadowed by studies emphasizing more traditional ones (Bass & Bass, 2008; Northouse, 2010; Yukl, 2013). Some authors have suggested that the study of collaboration in leadership has been marginalized within the literature (Gronn, 2008; Nohria & Khurana, 2010; Podolny, Khurana, & Besharov, 2010; Seers, Keller, & Wilkerson, 2003). Despite the lack of exposure, these approaches have sustained interest in both academic and practice communities and more recently are gaining increasing interest within the leadership literature (Wassenaar & Pearce, 2012). While empirical research remains at a nascent stage, theories are proliferating.

There is a concurrent conversation underway in the feminist, peace, and systems literatures about constructing power in broader terms than are explored in the traditional discourses (Karlberg, 2005). Part of that dialogue focuses on the need to challenge the generally accepted view of power as strictly an instrument of dominance, coercion, and conflict (Allen, 1999; Boulding, 1990; Fletcher, 2004; Karlberg, 2004,

2005). Power is a ubiquitous and animating force of all social worlds and is present whenever humans organize (Tjosvold & Wisse, 2009). This principle applies particularly to leadership. That is, to discuss leadership is to discuss power (Bass & Bass, 2008; Burns, 1978; Gardner, 1990; Northouse, 2010; Rost, 1993; Yukl, 2013). Youngs (2009) went further by suggesting that leadership is in fact a vehicle for power.

Given the importance of this relationship, it is curious that discussions of power have largely been avoided within the leadership literature that addresses collaborative approaches (Bolden, 2011; Denis, Langley, & Sergi, 2012; Gronn, 2008). An explanation may be found in Kanter's observation that power is considered to be a "dirty word" (1994, p. 1) or, in K. J. Gergen's view, that it is a "rhetorically hot" (1995, p. 29) topic. Dirty, hot, or otherwise, the exploration of power within the context of this approach to leadership is essential if our understanding is to be advanced in meaningful ways.

A few authors have recognized this gap. For example, Gronn (2008) pondered whether society has merely entered the age of distribution, where the concept of distribution is being explored and applied across multiple phenomena such as information systems, knowledge, cognition, decision-making, and learning systems. He noted that the concept of leadership, and by inference, power might be equally affected by this paradigm shift toward distribution. Bolden, Petrov, and Gosling (2009) promoted the importance of examining power dynamics within distributed forms of leadership to understand how they "enable or constrain particular forms of engagement in leadership practice" (p. 260). Fletcher (2004) warned that the transformative potential of contemporary leadership theories may not be met if we do not explore the deeper issues behind their "complex gender and power dynamics" (p. 656). At a societal level, Karlberg (2005) observed that "Western-liberal discourses of power and the social practices associated with them are proving inadequate to the task of creating a peaceful, just, and sustainable social order" (p. 1). Leadership is one such social practice. From these perspectives, it would appear that the exploration of collaborative leadership and power is an important one.

The following sections explain the purpose of this study and the research question that guides this work. The inspiration for this research, definitions of key terms, conceptual framework, research methodologies, and underpinning assumptions are also considered.

Purpose

The purpose of this study is to expand our understanding of collaborative approaches to leadership within an organizational context by exploring how leaders who practice this approach construct power.

Research Question

The research question guiding this study asks how leaders who are identified as collaborative construct power.

Inspiration

My interest in this topic is rooted in a lifelong pursuit of fairness, equity, and social justice. As a newly minted business professional I was confronted by the contradictions of organizational life. I heard leaders boldly pronounce themselves autocrats, unconcerned with the contradiction presented by our living in a democratic society that enabled their having such choice. Many sought status, prestige, and power, typically at the expense of others. I frequently witnessed the underutilization of human potential and wasted effort as people focused their energies on trying to either please or resist authority.

I have also experienced the opposite, working with leaders whose primary focus is on building individual and organizational capacity. They inspire, motivate, and collaborate. More recently, I have had the privilege of serving on teams and committees where like-minded peers push the boundaries of prevailing leadership paradigms by aspiring to lead collaboratively in an environment of equalized power. It has been my experience that such an approach can expand human potential, promote innovation and creativity, and forge group unity. As a result, I was inspired to explore this concept of leadership through formal research and learn how to both expand awareness generally and to integrate learning about this approach to leadership into my consulting work and writing.

Definition of Terms

Three terms of collaborative leadership, power, and construct warrant clarification.

Collaborative Leadership

For ease of reference, the term *collaborative leadership* has been employed throughout this study, except where shared, collective, distributed, and relational leadership literatures are discussed. In these instances, the term employed in the literature is used. Similar to the broader field of leadership, definitions for collaborative approaches have proliferated over time (Bolden, 2011). While collaborative leadership is not the most prevalent label employed within the leadership literature, it has a presence (Finch, 1977; Mendenhall & Marsh, 2010; Raelin, 2006). The term as it is used here represents a composite of several.[1]

There are two reasons for choosing to use the term collaborative leadership. First, other labels used in the literature do not adequately reflect all that is occurring when leaders employ a collaborative approach. Second, the term tends to be invoked by leaders who practice collaboration with their followers. A more detailed discussion of why the term collaborative leadership was chosen is provided in Chapter 2.

For this study, collaborative leadership is defined as a dynamic, interactive process that occurs between two or more people, the purpose of which is to facilitate decision-making and shared agreement on direction, alignment to goals, and a commitment to action. This definition derives from two primary sources: Pearce and Conger's (2003) definition of shared leadership and Drath et al.'s (2008) leadership outcomes of their integrative theory of leadership.

Power

The interest in this study is in social power that is expressed through leadership in an organizational context. Social power is defined as "the degree of influence that an individual or organization has among their peers and within their society as a whole" (*Social power*, n.d.). For the sake of efficiency and ease of reading, the term *power* is used throughout the study. In this study, power is regarded as a ubiquitous and benign social force that can be harnessed and transformed by individuals who hold the necessary capacity to do so. Capacity means having the ability to contain, perform, experience, or comprehend something. A social force is understood to be "an element of society which has the capability of causing cultural change or influences people" (*Social force*, n.d.). Individuals are understood to exercise choice in terms of how they animate power. For example, their intention may be to have it serve as a coercive and constraining force; as a productive force; or as a mutualistic, integrative, and transformative force.

Construct

Because this is a study that considers how leaders construct power, it calls for a common understanding of how the term *construct* is being applied. To construct is to learn (Berger & Luckmann, 1966/1991; Hein, 1999), and learning or meaning making is the process by which humans navigate life. This study views the process of construction to require both thought and action before a concept is fully constituted (Greeno, Collins, & Resnick, 1996).

Conceptual Framework

This study is situated at the intersection of the four literatures: collaborative leadership, power, agency and communion, and constructivism (see Figure 1). The following overview briefly introduces these literatures and connects them to the research question and to the methodologies that guide this inquiry. It also discusses the purpose in employing a multi-methodological approach. All four of these literatures are reviewed in greater detail in Chapter 2.

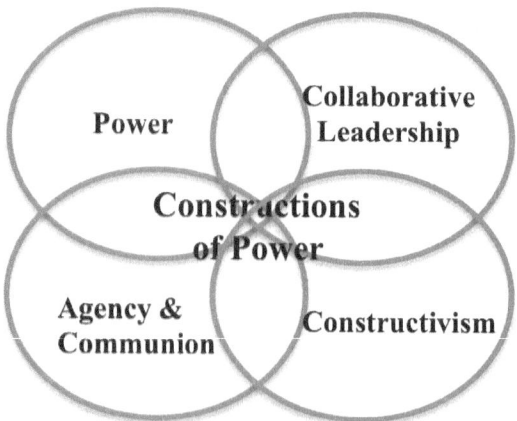

Figure 1. Conceptual Framework for the study

Collaborative Leadership

The first literature within the conceptual framework is collaborative leadership. As this is a study of collaborative leadership, it is imperative to explore this topic. While there are growing numbers of leadership theories that suggest collaboration between leaders and followers, they do not represent a unified field. The most frequently studied are *shared* and *distributed* leadership (Bolden, 2011; Fitzsimons, James, & Denyer, 2011). Also of significance are *collective* (Friedrich, Vessey, Schuelke, Ruark, & Mumford, 2009) and *relational* leadership theories (Uhl-Bien, 2006; Uhl-Bien & Ospina, 2012). Denis et al. (2012) referred to this field as "the collective leadership phenomenon" (p. 212). In their analysis, Denis et al. identified clear distinctions across the various theories. However, they also identified one common feature: Research on the use of power in collaborative leadership is lacking. This is important as the very nature of these collaborative theories suggests a distinction in how leaders think about and use power when compared to more traditional leadership approaches.

Each of the collaborative leadership theories can be categorized as either *entitative* or *relational* (Dachler & Hosking, 1995; Fitzsimons, 2012; Ospina & Uhl-Bien, 2012). Entitative theories are grounded in a modernist paradigm and focus on the individual. Shared and collective leadership theories are considered to be entitative. How leaders use power in their relationship with followers is understood to be the product of their thoughts and therefore the focus of study is on the individual. Alternatively, relational theories are informed by a postmodernist paradigm that views thoughts and behaviors as the products of social engagement. Actors are secondary. The primary focus is on the process of engagement. The construction of both leadership and power are understood to emerge out of the dynamics of relationships. Distributed and relational leadership are encompassed by this category.

While this is primarily a study of how individual leaders construct power, and would therefore be considered an entitative study, both lenses are applied in an effort to obtain a more holistic perspective on such constructions within the two organizations studied.

Power

As this study explores the construction of power by collaborative leaders, understanding the power literature is as important as the collaborative leadership literature. The power literature tends to emphasize exercising dominance over others to the exclusion of other manifestations of power. This literature has influenced the study of leadership to the extent that the leadership literature also tends to define power in these same limited terms. In the present study, a case will be made for viewing power as a neutral force that can manifest in multiple forms. These are dominance (power-over), individual capability (power-to), and mutualistic (power-with). How power is manifest becomes a matter of choice.

Agency and Communion

Agency and communion are terms coined by Bakan (1966) to represent two primary motivations in life. Agency manifests in behaviors directed toward achievement of personal goals conveyed as ambition, competence, and self-protection. This motivation is most commonly associated with power as dominance. Communion is defined by behaviors that support building and maintaining relationships such as cooperativeness, moral integrity, warmth, and focusing on others (Abele & Wojciszke, 2007; Ybarra et al., 2008). Communion tends to be linked with intimacy and relational behavior and is not generally associated with power. Power in intimate relationships is understood to be rooted in issues of the ego and is therefore associated with agency. A compelling avenue for understanding how leaders construct power is to consider how they manifest agency and communion when they enact collaborative leadership. As indicated above, in the review of the power literature, this study proposes that how power is manifest is a matter of choice. Understanding how an individual balances agency and communion is thought to be linked to how they choose to manifest power.

Constructivism

The construction of a concept or meaning making requires both thought and action. In order to understand how collaborative leaders construct power, the researcher therefore needs to explore both the individual's thoughts and his or her intersubjective or relational actions. Constructivist theories explain how humans generate knowledge and meaning about reality (Berger & Luckmann, 1966/1991; Hein, 1999). Two constructivist theories guide this study: cognitive and social constructionism. Each is underpinned by a distinct paradigm about how knowledge is generated. Cognitive theory places the emphasis on individuals and how they perceive, interpret, and judge the world around them in the course of meaning making. It considers processes in which the individual is the active participant in meaning making (Fairhurst & Grant, 2010; K. J. Gergen, 1995; Greeno et al., 1996; C. C. Liu & I Ju, 2010).

Social constructionist theory informs the relational perspective. Meaning is the product of relationships and not the possession of individuals (Dachler & Hosking, 1995; Fairhurst

& Grant, 2010; M. Gergen, 1995). Social constructionism emphasizes meaning making through social engagement where constructing knowledge is a shared process (M. Gergen, 1995). That is, socially constructed meaning making takes place through intersubjective action, typically dialogue, where two or more people co-construct and confirm meaning (Greeno et al., 1996).

Methodology Overview

Methodologies are tethered to epistemologies. How one will study a given phenomenon is determined by how one understands what constitutes knowledge (Corbin & Strauss, 2008; Creswell, 2013; Crotty, 1998; Guba & Lincoln, 2005; Maxwell, 2005; Morgan & Smircich, 1980; Richards & Morse, 2007). As a result, researchers would typically apply one or another methodology. For example, researchers would generally employ a methodology informed by either cognitive theory or social constructionist theory but not both. The reason is that the methodologies that stem from these two differing theories are informed by epistemologies that are thought to be incommensurate with each other. However, insights gained from one perspective can be complementary to the other to the extent that each will shed light on different aspects of the same phenomenon.

Two distinct methodologies are employed in this study, each rooted in a different epistemology. The fundamental conflict between these two approaches and how it is resolved is discussed in Chapter 3. The current discussion offers an introduction to them. The inquiry process employed in this study is guided by an epistemological stance that holds that an objective reality exists and can be accessed, even if in limited terms. It also contec activity that occurs at two levels:

individually and collectively. That is, individuals think or apply their cognitive abilities to make sense of the world around them and they also engage in the co-construction of meaning (Fairhurst & Grant, 2010; M. Gergen, 1995).

Data were collected through individual interviews, group observation, and analyses of organizational systems and structures. Interviews explore individual thoughts about power, while group observation reveals the social construction of meaning through relationship dynamics. These data are supplemented by insights gained from a review of organization systems and structures. Systems and structures are artifacts of thought and action and provide evidence of how the cognitive and social constructions of power are reinforced. They are "constituting elements of human activity" (Spillane & Sherer, 2004, p. 7).

In terms of methodology, this study employs a qualitative approach. A phenomenological lens is applied to explore the interview data, and an ethnographic lens is used to reveal how power manifests within the organizations. Both group observations and organizational systems and structures were analyzed using the ethnographic lens.

Assumptions

There are three assumptions guiding this study. The first concerns the process of developing robust data. This inquiry explores leadership in two distinct organizations where collaborative leadership is intentionally practiced. Typically, for comparison purposes, the qualitative researcher would study examples that do not reflect the phenomenon under consideration in order to enhance the credibility and dependability of research outcomes. However, such an approach presents difficulties for this type of inquiry. It has become de rigueur to be viewed as collaborative in one's approach to leadership. Leadership labelled as *top-down* is no longer in vogue. Thus, it is doubtful people would consent to being the counterpoint in a study of collaborative leadership.

The two organizations under consideration in this study are distinct. One is engaged in the work of generating and sustaining multiple forms of inter-organizational collaborations at local and international levels. The nature of their work ranges from social justice to business effectiveness projects. While the second organization is a more traditional enterprise, it is built on a cooperative governance structure and invests in learning about how to apply collaboration for business effectiveness. I believe that studying more than one organization will enhance data credibility and dependability. Furthermore, the outcomes of studying two exemplary organizations can advance theory and practice as effectively as comparing one organization that is against one that is not. These organizations are considered exemplary within the context of collaborative leadership to the extent that they are purposefully learning to apply this approach.

The second assumption concerns my personal thoughts about leadership and power. By virtue of my past experience and interest in studying this topic, I consider a collaborative approach to leadership to be an effective one, particularly in the context of complex environments. A diversity of perspectives, made possible through collaboration, may offer an efficacious option where solutions are not obvious and require innovative and creative thinking. Both through a review of the literature, and my personal experience, collaborative leaders also tend to forge group unity, which brings with it important elements of social justice that are not possible in more traditional approaches. I also believe that power can be expressed and manifested in broader terms than coercion and dominance.

I have assumed that collaborative leaders construct power in a manner different enough from traditional leaders for this research to be worthwhile.

My third assumption is reflective of the debates about whether or not a phenomenon can be two different things at the same time, rather like the duck/rabbit picture (Wittgenstein, 1986) that challenges the dichotomous worldview. I believe that phenomena can be both/and, as in leadership can be *both* hierarchical *and* heterarchical at the same time. Throughout this research, it has been essential for me to be aware of and to bracket my assumptions (Richards & Morse, 2007).

Figure 2. Duck/rabbit optical illusion. This ambiguous drawing was made famous by Ludwig von Wittgenstein in his *Philosophical Investigations*. He employed this device to demonstrate how there may be more than one way of seeing a phenomenon. This picture is from the 23 October 1892 issue of *Fliegende Blätter* (https://en.wikipedia.org/wiki/Fliegende_Bl%C3%A4tter).

Significance

This study adds to both scholarship and practice. From a scholarship perspective, it brings together into one conversation two currently separate discourses on collaborative leadership and power. In doing so, it generates insights that specifically address a current void in the literature. This study also contributes to discourses on leadership and power by offering evidence of broader definitions and applications currently in use by leaders. From a practice perspective, there is a transformative frame to this work (Creswell, 2013). As it contributes to an evolving discourse on how we think and talk about the dynamics of power in leadership, the findings are expected to aid in advancing our understanding of leadership.

The Fielding doctoral program is founded on a scholar-practitioner framework with an objective of guiding researchers in learning how to move theory into practice. The insights from this study are transferable to practice, particularly executive coaching, leadership development initiatives, and organization development work. Finally, multi-methodological research is a relatively recent phenomenon, particularly in the leadership literature. This study adds to our learning about how to develop complementary insights through the application of more than one research methodology, each of which is informed by a distinct epistemology or philosophy of what constitutes human knowledge.

Summary

While the leadership literature is already extensive, the opportunities and challenges of an ever-advancing society demand that we continuously increase and expand our knowledge about this important aspect of human organization. Although the literature on collaborative leadership is increasing, the lack of studies that explore power leaves a critical gap. This study endeavors to address that gap and make a useful contribution toward filling it.

The purpose of this study is to gain a broader perspective on the construction of power by leaders who have been identified as collaborative in their approach. In this sense, it is an entitative study. However, it also assumes a relational lens to the extent that it explores how power manifests in relationships between leaders and followers. The following chapter reviews the literature relevant to this study and identifies a gap between collaborative leadership and power, confirming the importance of pursuing this work.

CHAPTER TWO

REVIEW OF THE LITERATURE

Leadership has become a central theme in the social sciences and of widespread concern in society at large (Parry & Bryman, 2006; Van Vugt, Hogan, & Kaiser, 2008). Much is known about this subject, and multiple studies explore its trajectory (Bass & Bass, 2008; Gibb, 1954/1969; Hernandez et al., 2011; House & Aditya, 1997; Parry & Bryman, 2006; Yukl, 2013). However, there remains a great deal to understand (House & Aditya, 1997). One topic that warrants further study is the relationship between leadership and power.

Whether or not it is acknowledged, most leadership studies consider some aspect of power. Tjosvold and Wisse (2009) observe that power is a ubiquitous and animating force of social worlds that is present whenever humans organize. Kellerman (2012) posits that the study of leadership "more than anything else . . . is about the devolution of power—from those on top to those down below" (p. 3). And many scholars note that leadership and power are thought to be synonymous (Bass & Bass, 2008; Burns, 1978; Gardner, 1990; Northouse, 2010; Rost, 1993; Yukl, 2013). In fact, this idea is so prevalent that these two phenomena are frequently conflated.

The prevailing discourse in the leadership literature

assumes leaders exercise power *over* others. Because they are hierarchically higher, leaders are therefore understood to hold greater power. The two primary foci of studies that do explore leadership and power are the individual power of leaders, and the manner in which leaders empower others. The leader is typically positioned as a dominating figure with followers submissive to this role. Empowerment is portrayed as something that leaders do to followers, rather than viewing it as a dynamic instrument of capacity building.

Because power is central to leadership, studies that explore power in the context of collaborative leadership are essential for theory advancement. This review contends that the singular construct of power as dominance or power over others is not in alignment with the phenomenon of collaborative leadership, and that broader constructions are warranted. These broader constructions are inclusive of mutualistic power defined as an integrative and transformative use of power with others. It is further argued that power is a capacity rather than a possession, and as such can be expressed in multiple ways beyond dominance. This study proposes that how power is exercised is a matter of choice and that choice is influenced by how one balances one's sense of agency with his or her communal motivations. It is argued that the concept of empowerment practiced by collaborative leaders transcends how it is defined within the traditional leadership literature. In essence, the capacity for power is inherent to the individual and therefore needs to be drawn out rather than gifted. Finally, it is argued that power and hierarchy have been conflated in the literature where power has been constructed as dominance. When these two concepts are disaggregated, it becomes possible to envision broader constructions of power even within hierarchical structures.

This study is situated at the intersection of the four literatures:

collaborative leadership, power, agency and communion, and constructivism. This chapter offers a critical review of each of these literatures, connects them to the research question informing this study, and demonstrates the gap in research between the collaborative leadership and power literatures. The review of the agency and communion literature elucidates the choice leaders have in how they express power and asserts that striving to balance these two behavioral modalities results in a preference for mutualistic constructions. The constructivism literature demonstrates the value of exploring both individual thoughts and intersubjective relations to gain a more holistic perspective on how collaborative leaders construct power.

Collaborative Leadership Theories

The following discussion provides an overview of the leadership literature that explores collaborative approaches, followed by a review of the central issues as they relate to power. It begins with a historical perspective on this literature, followed by an overview of the predominate theories. This section concludes with a discussion of the complementarity between entitative and relational lenses and a critique of the collaborative leadership literature.

Origins

Beliefs about the origins of collaborative leadership theories are varied. For example, some have suggested that it represents a progression of the concept of empowerment and/or relational theories such as Leader Member Exchange or LMX (Yukl, 2013). Others viewed this literature to be an entirely new line of research (Parry & Bryman, 2006). The concept of sharing or distributing leadership beyond a single leader is frequently attributed to Gibb (1954/1969).

However, others considered deeper roots. Gronn (2008) posited that it is possible to trace theory development throughout the 20th century. Pearce and Conger (2003) proposed that theory development parallels individual leadership theory. There are mentions of collaborative forms of leadership throughout the last 100 years of leadership study. Mary Parker Follett emphasized one such approach in the 1920s (Graham, 2003; Héon, Davis, Jones-Patulli, & Damart, 2014; Metcalf & Urwick, 1940/2013). Lewin, Lippitt, and White (1939) also identified a collaborative approach in their landmark study of climates of leadership. In fact, collaborative leadership may be as ancient as the notion of leadership itself. Evidence points to the North American Blackfoot (Bass & Bass, 2008) and the Australian Aboriginal tribes (Sveiby, 2011) engaging in collaborative practices.

In spite of its extensive lineage, collaborative approaches to leadership have remained a liminal area of inquiry residing at the periphery of mainstream research in the contemporary social sciences. However, interest appears to be growing, evidenced by increasing numbers of empirical studie[2] As interest accrues, labels proliferate. Currently, the most frequently employed ones are *shared* (Crevani et al., 2007; Ensley, Hmieleski, & Pearce, 2006; Pearce & Conger, 2003), *collective* (Friedrich et al., 2009), *distributed* (Gronn, 2008; Spillane, Halverson, & Diamond, 2001), and *relational* (Uhl-Bien, 2006; Uhl-Bien et al., 2007). A distinct community of researchers represents each theory, and in some cases theories are focused on specific sectors and/or geographic regions. For example, studies of shared leadership have largely been conducted in business, medical, and nursing settings in the United States. Distributed leadership has mainly been explored in the educational sector by researchers in the United States, Australia, and Britain. Most of the research and theory development have been generated within the last 25 years, and the majority of the work was produced within the last 15 years.

Evidence of an expanding interest can also be found elsewhere. First, the number of meta-studies is increasing. Fitzsimons et al. (2011) compared distributed and shared leadership theories and the varying approaches to their study. Bennett, Wise, Woods, and Harvey (2003) offered an overview of the literature on distributed leadership to date. Bolden (2011) built on this work and compared the conceptual underpinnings of distributed, shared, collaborative, collective, and democratic leadership theories. Yammarino et al. (2012) explored the common themes across what they term collectivist theories including team, network, shared, complexity, and collective leadership. Denis et al. (2012) reviewed, synthesized, and contrasted what they refer to as *leadership in the plural*. Many of these meta-studies formed part of special editions of academic journals dedicated to collaborative approaches.

Another indicator of the growing interest is a rapidly expanding number of websites within the practice community that mention these various collaborative approaches. In fact, practice appears to be outpacing theory development. A recent Google search produced millions of hits[4] for each theory, where the largest number of sites was from the practice community.

Finally, and potentially most importantly, in the latter part of the 20th century, a significant number of institutions in multiple sectors, both regional and international, embraced the need for collaboration.[5] Well-known examples include the European Union, the G8 and G20, and the United Nations. While there have been, and continue to be, challenges, this progression appears to be gaining momentum.

The following section offers an overview of the predominant collaborative leadership theories within the literature. Before proceeding, an important distinction between these theories needs to be highlighted. A discussion of their complementarity follows the overview.

Entitative and Relational Lenses

All collaborative leadership theories are essentially relational in nature. That is, there is a relationship between leaders and followers. However, our understanding of the nature of that relationship may differ, depending upon our worldview. Two categories for understanding these relationships are entitative and relational (Fitzsimons, 2012; Uhl-Bien & Ospina, 2012).

The entitative stance is rooted in a modernist worldview where relationships are understood to be the product of distinct entities or individuals who engage with one another. This study is an exploration of how individual leaders think about power in the context of their relationships with followers. Collaborative leadership theories that fall under the entitative rubric are related in the notions of there being individual actors who are identified as leaders, of leaders being more collaborative with followers when compared to more traditional approaches to leadership, and of leadership being dispersed among followers in some way beyond the individual leader. Thoughts and behaviors are understood to be tangible phenomena that are knowable and can be measured. Individuals are considered to be discrete and separate beings, and being is believed to precede relating. Descartes' famous "I think, therefore I am" (Descartes, 2008) assertion could be the byline of this stance.

Relational leadership theories are rooted in a postmodernist worldview, founded on social constructionist theory. That is, thoughts and behaviors are viewed as products of social engagement. The introduction of relational leadership theory is part of a larger movement in academic circles referred to as a "relational turn" (Uhl-Bien & Ospina, 2012). Relational theory considers the "process of social construction produced through relationship" (Uhl-Bien & Ospina, 2012, p. 7). Relating precedes being, as individuals are defined by and through their relationships. All action is considered to be transactional, as more than one person will always be implicated in the action. The byline for this stance might be *through relationship we become*.

Collaborative Leadership Theories

Having outlined the fundamental distinctions between entitative and relational theories, it is now possible to review the predominant collaborative theories in the literature and highlight their fundamental differences against this backdrop. The primary leadership theories encompassed by the entitative category are shared and collective leadership. The principal leadership theories included in the relational category are distributed and relational leadership. It is important to note that these categorizations are not always self-evident in the literature and scholars occasionally conflate these two schools of thought. More recently, a dialogue has been launched within the literature that promotes a dialogue among perspectives (Uhl-Bien & Ospina, 2012) and considers whether or not the two lenses are complementary (Uhl-Bien & Ospina, 2012). That dialogue is discussed following the overview of the leading leadership theories.

Shared leadership. Pearce and Conger (2003) launched a formal dialogue on this topic with their book *Shared Leadership: Reframing the Hows and Whys of Leadership*. They defined shared leadership as "a dynamic, interactive influence process among individuals in groups for which the objective is to lead one another to the achievement of group or organizational goals or both" (p. 1). Pearce and Conger's stated intention for this work was to explore alternative forms of leadership beyond the hierarchical models typical of the leadership literature (Pearce, Conger, & Locke, 2008). While the conversation about shared leadership has expanded considerably, its roots are firmly planted in this early discourse.

Pearce and Conger (Pearce, Conger, & Locke, 2008) proposed that shared leadership is an integrated model that encompasses multiple configurations including top-down, bottom-up, and lateral influences. The individual leading may shift, depending upon the issue at hand as leadership is understood to represent a capacity rather than a position (Pearce & Conger, 2003). Leadership teams can form at any level of the organization, from deep inside an organization to the senior management level. Pearce, Manz, and Sims (2008) posited that shared leadership could be complementary to vertical leadership. They proposed a model of leadership intended to mitigate the potential for corrupt behaviors, advocating for leadership to be viewed as a process rather than a role that can be performed by multiple individuals. In their model the CEO, or highest-level leader, models and promotes shared leadership behaviors within the top management team.

Pearce, Manz, et al. (2008) are essentially promoting the coexistence of hierarchy and heterarchy. A hierarchy is a stratum of positions, ranked one upon the other where each level is subordinate to the one above. A heterarchy is a network of connected positions that does not require a permanent upper layer. Pearce, Manz, et al. proposed that in an integrated model such as this leaders will tend to focus their sense of agency toward the greater good, thereby mitigating the potential for corrupt behaviors within the group. They also noted that empirical evidence for shared leadership "has consistently linked it with positive organizational outcomes" (p.

356).

Collective leadership. Friedrich et al. (2009) developed an integrative framework intended to blend the growing body of literature that explores the distribution of the leadership role. Collective leadership focuses on how multiple individuals can assume the role of leadership, and how this role can traverse the boundary between leader(s) and teams. Friedrich et al. defined collective leadership as "a dynamic leadership process in which a defined leader, or set of leaders, selectively utilize skills and expertise within a network, effectively distributing elements of the leadership role as the situation or problem at hand requires" (p. 933).

Similar to shared leadership, collective and vertical leadership are not necessarily mutually exclusive concepts and can be complementary to one another (Friedrich et al., 2009). Leaders continue to be important actors, whether as individuals or as a collective. Friedrich et al. (2009) suggested central tenets for success in collaborative structures: All members need to be willing to share information, to collaborate, and to engage in collective decision-making; there must be trust between leaders and followers; and dissent and feedback must be possible without consequence if groupthink is to be avoided.

Another similarity to shared leadership is the resemblance to the work of Mary Parker Follett (Metcalf & Urwick, 1940/2013), particularly in the notion of the leader emerging dependant upon the needs of the situation. Different issues and needs arise over time, requiring distinct skills and abilities. Leaders consult followers on complex problems and on problem-solving implementation, evaluation, and revisions. Such consultations not only benefit the organization, but also serve to build the capacity of followers to engage in these activities.

Friedrich et al. (2009) proposed that individuals could assume a leadership role opportunistically or in a planned manner, as a result of leader intervention in response to situational needs. The authors observed that the literature tends to view team members as equal and does not make distinctions. They noted that in reality, individuals contribute unique characteristics and a diversity of skill sets. Thus, not all individuals will be equal to all tasks or issues.

Distributed leadership. Distributed leadership is the first of two relational theories to be explored. Gibb (1954/1969) is generally cited as the first author to use the term distributed leadership, describing it as "a group quality, as a set of functions that must be carried out by the group" (p. 215). In recent years, theory development has proliferated to the point where Thorpe et al. (2011) observed the lack of a universally accepted definition. Spillane and Sherer (2004) also commented that distributed leadership tends to mean different things to different people. Spillane and Sherer (2004) viewed distributed leadership not as a theory, but as a lens for exploring leadership practice. Spillane (2005) explained that distributed leadership is the practice of leadership from the perspective of the interactions between and among people within a given situation rather than the practice of leadership as a product of a leader's knowledge and skill.

Alternatively, Gronn (2002) separated distributed leadership into two configurations. The first was inspired by Gibb's (1954/1969) concept of a leadership complex. By shifting the emphasis away from the individual leader, some or all members of the group become potential leaders. No one person is seen as more valuable and anyone may take on a leadership role at any given time. This description bears a resemblance to Mary Parker Follett's (Metcalf & Urwick, 1940/2013) *law of the situation* (p. 59) and to Pearce and Conger's (2003) shared leadership theory, which was inspired by Follett. Gronn described the second configuration as "concertive action" (p. 429). Members engage in what he described as conjoint action, meaning that leaders coordinate their plans with their peers. He identified three types of concertive action: spontaneous collaborative engagement, intuitive responses that increase over time as relationships develop, and action that becomes institutionalized as relationships are normalized.

Similar to shared leadership, arguments have been made in favor of blending hierarchical and heterarchical structures (Gronn, 2008, 2009; Youngs, 2009). Gronn (2009) commented on the "pointlessness of pitting focused and distributed approaches to leadership against one another" (p. 383). He conceded that both individual and distributed leadership must be taken into consideration in exploring patterns of relationships. Despite a desire to shift the focus of research away from individual leaders and toward leadership within a given situation, he noted that individual leaders continue to hold a place of importance in studies. Gronn referred to this combination as hybrid leadership and recommended that leadership configurations or patterns of relationships become the unit of analysis.

Relational Leadership. Relational leadership theory by its very name is understood to fall under the relational rubric. While a relatively recent phenomenon to be explored (Dachler & Hosking, 1995; Uhl-Bien, 2006), relational leadership theory has clear antecedents (Fairhurst & Grant, 2010). Hunt and Dodge (2001) identified social network theory, leader-member exchange, lateral/representational/distributive, collective, and systems theory as precursors. Uhl-Bien (2006) launched the current dialogue on relational leadership theory. She presented it as a framework for studying leadership as a social influence process through which new social order and its attendant change are constructed. Examples of the types of change that are of interest include actions, attitudes, behaviors, beliefs, and so forth. Uhl-Bien and Ospina (2012) described relational leadership theory (RLT) as a means for "viewing the invisible threads that connect actors" (p. xx). The focus shifts away from the individual actors and toward the dynamics of the relationship between leaders and followers. While actors are understood to exist, they are not the primary focus (Uhl-Bien, 2006).

Bradbury and Lichtenstein (2000) explained that "knowing occurs between two subjects or phenomena simultaneously, therefore we must attend to the multiple meanings and perspectives that continuously emerge" (p. 552). Fitzsimons (2012) stated that relationships are not vehicles for knowledge or influencing. Rather, "they are processes in which individuals come to experience themselves, others, and other organizational phenomena through the ongoing flow of intersubjective meaning making in different cultural and social contexts" (p. 155). Leadership need not be restricted to hierarchical positions; it can also be distributed throughout the organization and occur within a given context (Uhl-Bien, 2006).

For example, Raelin's (2012) notion of *leaderful* organizations presented leadership as a process that emerges from the dialogue and deliberation between leaders and followers. All parties are thought to have relational equality in the conversation regardless of their position within the hierarchy. In this sense, his theory of leadership was democratically inspired. Crevani et al.'s (2007) exploration of a postheroic theory of leadership identified the coexistence of hierarchical and heterarchical leadership. Organizational members continue to co-construct leadership as a unitary command (Pearce & Manz, 2005), that is, leadership exercised by a single person, while at the same time "strive to find leadership procedures that involve many people and make use of the diverse competences that exist" (Crevani et al., 2007, p. 61).

Denis et al. (2012) noted that relational leadership theories contribute to the "perennial interrogation about the nature of leadership" (p. 254). Rooted in their postmodern stance, these theories provide a lens for critiquing leadership in a way that no other approach offers. As Denis et al. noted, relational theories offer such possibilities through "philosophical inquiries, empirical studies of what, on a daily basis, leadership is about, reconceptualizations of leadership, ethical concerns, questioning of leadership discourse, etc." (p. 254).

A Dialogue Among Entitative and Relational Theories

Returning briefly to the earlier discussion about entitative and relational theories, scholars have begun to explore how theories encompassed by these two lenses may be complementary. As stated earlier, entitative theories focus on individuals. In a leadership context this would include a study of leaders and their engagement with followers. Relational theories are concerned with what is occurring within the relationships. Individuals are incidental to the extent that the focus of an inquiry is shifted away from any one person's contribution and toward the dynamic that is occurring among the participants.

Recently, Uhl-Bien and Ospina (2012) launched a dialogue among scholars who explore leadership from each of the entitative and relational stances. While no definitive conclusions were reached, their efforts firmly established the importance of both lenses. They concluded that this is messy work that requires an open mind and a willingness to explore issues across paradigms or worldviews, rather like the duck/

rabbit concept (Wittgenstein, 1986). They declared that "the 'relational turn' has arrived" (p. xix) and that a relational lens needs to take an equal place of importance alongside the still dominant entitative lens if a comprehensive understanding of leadership is to be attained. As Pearce and Conger (Pearce, Conger, et al., 2008) noted, "the crux of this issue is the challenge of integrating the view of leadership as a role performed by an individual with the view of leadership as a social process" (p. 626).

Critique of Collaborative Leadership Theories

The field of study of collaborative approaches to leadership is far from unified. To begin with, there is a lack of clarity about the use of terms across the various streams. Denis et al. (2012) observed that some are used loosely and are occasionally interchanged. For example, while most scholars viewed distributed leadership as a singular theory, expressions of it can differ from one study to another (Bolden, 2011). Thorpe et al. (2011) defined distributed leadership as "a variety of configurations which emerge from the exercise of influence that produces interdependent and conjoint action" (p. 241). This lack of clarity creates confusion about the field.

Aside from the challenges in the literature, from a practice perspective not everyone will want to engage in collaborative practices. Not every leader will want to dilute his or her power, not every follower equally desires power, and not everyone will have the same capacity to access and utilize it. If not implemented with caution, organizations may continue with unequal distributions of power, only in new constellations. A shift to collaborative leadership presents a tall order for transformation where traditional vertically structured organizations are concerned. This raises questions as to whether only newly formed organizations are realistic spawning grounds for collaborative leadership.

While there are numerous distinctions and a few similarities across all of these collaborative leadership theories, there is one common feature. There is a lack of treatment of power (Denis et al., 2012).

Power

The second literature of importance to this study is power. The literature that explores power in the context of leadership is juxtaposed to and shaped by the Western discourse about power (Karlberg, 2005). Thus, it is incumbent upon the researcher to consider the broader power literature in any inquiry into leadership and power. The following is a review of that broader literature followed by a discussion of its relationship to leadership. A further discussion of the gap between the collaborative leadership and power literatures closes out this chapter.

Power is a central concept within the social sciences (Boulding, 1990; Haugaard & Clegg, 2009), and has been for as long as theories of social order have existed (Haugaard & Clegg, 2009). The primary power debates revolve around how it is constituted, how it is exercised, what the vehicles of power are, and whether or not it is a human capacity. This study touches on each of these debates, but the central concerns are with how power is constituted, and the question of whether or not it is a capacity.

How Power is Constituted

Efforts to define power have not advanced far beyond Dahl's (1957) assessment of efforts. He explained,

Most people have an intuitive notion of what it means. But scientists have not yet formulated a statement of the concept of power that is rigorous enough to be of use in the systematic study of this important social phenomenon. (p. 201)

Beginning with Weber (1964), power associated with leadership has typically been viewed as a form of dominance, where one party exercises his or her will or power over another to get what he or she wants "despite resistance" (p. 152). Since then, Weber's stance has influenced how power is conceived (Dowding, 2008; Göhler, 2009; Lukes, 2005; Pfohl, 2008). For example, Lukes (2005) posited that consensual perspectives of power are of limited value in that they are revisionist and therefore out of alignment with traditional conceptualizations. His concern was that a focus on consensual power overshadows and draws attention away from the dominance model. As Karlberg (2005) observed, Lukes' argument overshadows other concepts of power by singularly promoting the dominance perspective. Wartenberg (1990) also defended the exclusive study of dominance. Unlike Lukes, he acknowledged differing conceptions of power. However, he defended the exclusive study of dominance because, he contends, it alone offers a critical perspective by shedding light on inequities and therefore on social injustices.

While critique plays an important role in the research enterprise, generating new possibilities is equally important. At minimum, both dominance and mutualistic forms of power need to be explored. For example, if one studied only the British actions in the conflict with the people of India at the time of Mahatma Gandhi, the world might never have known about the power of collective nonviolent protest. This use of power has since animated numerous movements such as the American Civil Rights Movement, the fight against apartheid in South Africa, the Arab Spring, and the Occupy Movement.[7]

Another argument in favor of broader explorations of power lies in the fact that constructing the present based solely on tradition can restrain innovative thinking and preclude redefinitions that might better respond to current exigencies. As Pfohl (2008) commented, "the tradition of all the dead generations weigh on the brain of the living" (p. 5). He promoted a reflexive examination of our understanding of concepts such as power to avoid the risk of meanings becoming rituals that are mistaken for reality. Morriss (2002) was similarly supportive of such broader perspective taking. He posited that if power can only be exercised *over* people, then using a neutral definition would just as easily discover it, as it would if one used a definition of dominance.

Other scholars have equally made a case for defining power in broader terms. For example, Karlberg (2005) advocated for a "discourse intervention" (p. 1) to more clearly articulate the equally important mutualistic representations of power. His goal was to ensure that such constructions of power receive the same attention in theory building, as do models of dominance. Karlberg's purpose was also one of social justice. He posited that balancing the discourse among broader dimensions of power would alter how we shape our understanding of reality and therefore how we act in relationship to power. He observed that mutualistic forms of power are not new. However, they are of growing importance for enabling peaceful coexistence as the world becomes increasingly interdependent and, therefore, complex. His definition of mutualistic power is in alignment with the concept of power-with.

Locutions of Power. In addition to power as dominance, referred to as power-over, and mutualistic power, identified as power-with, there is a third locution of power called *power–to*. *Power-over*, *power-to*, and *power-with* are thus the three primary locutions employed in the literature to describe how power manifests. Western liberal societies tend to correlate power with coercion and conflict (Giddens, 1984). Within the political—philosophy, theory, science, and social science—literature, power is generally presented as a capacity of an individual that is used to dominate others (Arendt, 1969; Karlberg, 2005; Lukes, 2005; Wartenberg, 1990). This view is represented by the power-over term.

Pitkin (1972) introduced the notion that individuals have the power to accomplish actions independently. Described as having power-to, it is distinct from having power over others. The definition of power-to has since been a subject of much debate and has evolved to have multiple interpretations. Pitkin (1972) intended it as a form of consensual power that manifests in individual productive capacity that may or may not involve others in its exercise. She wrote,

> One may have power over another or others, and that sort of power is indeed relational . . . but he may have power to do or accomplish something all by himself, and that power is not relational at all; it may involve other people if what he has power to do is a social or political action, but it need not. (p. 277)

Thus, from Pitkin's (1972) perspective power-to represents productive capacity. It can be exercised individually or in concert with others as a form of exchange (Boulding, 1990). Next, feminists have applied this term to mean that an individual can "attain an end or series of ends that serve to challenge and/or subvert domination" (Allen, 1999, p. 126). In this interpretation, power-to is employed as a means of resistance to dominance. It can be exercised individually or in concert with others.

A third view holds that power-to can be applied as a

meta-concept that also incorporates the concept of power-over. Many theorists positioned the power-over orientation as a subset of power-to (Giddens, 1993; Göhler, 2009; Karlberg, 2005; Lukes, 2005; Morriss, 2002). Karlberg (2005) contended that one has *power to* exercise *power over* another. If this is true, then the concept of power-to can equally animate mutualistic forms of power such as power-with (Allen, 1999; Clegg & Haugaard, 2009). Thus, power-to can be considered as a meta-concept that incorporates both power-over and power-with.

Allen (1999) introduced the third locution of power-with into the contemporary power discourse. The term was first proposed by Follett (1940/2013) in the early part of the 20th century. She intended power-with to mean a consensual or mutualistic form of power that is integrative. That is, the pursuits of both leaders and followers become integrated as leaders use their power to influence followers, and followers reciprocate. Leaders enable followers to develop and exercise their power as appropriate to the situation and the capacity of the follower. In this way, a leader demonstrates the capacity to exercise power *with* others (Arendt, 1969; Boulding, 1990; Follett, 1940/2013; Karlberg, 2005). Boulding (1990) posited that the power- with offers the capacity to build, create, inspire, and bind. Although the power-with perspective can be found within the literature, it has been overshadowed by the power-over discourse.

References to the locution of power-with are sometimes found within the political and social science literatures, however the power-with discourse is mainly situated within the feminist, peace, and systems literatures (Karlberg, 2005).

The present study does not privilege one dimension of power over another. Doing so would reinforce a tendency in Western cultures to view the world in dichotomous terms. Rather, the stance adopted here is one of balancing, particularly the two predominant perspectives of power-over and power-with. This study does not reject the use of power-over or power as dominance in order to promote the importance of mutualistic power. Both are necessary. However, the contention here is that power as dominance must be used only for the greater good. Society continues to experience individual crime, aggressive acts on the part of groups and nations, corruption, and large-scale inequalities. All of these may require the exercise of power as dominance, at least as an initial response. When power as dominance is expressed in the best interests of others, it can serve a useful and valid purpose. However, as discussed earlier, broader constructions of power are essential if we are to counter the tendency to think of power only in these terms.

Power as Capacity

Power is frequently conceptualized in the leadership literature as a capacity, which is also understood to mean potential or ability (Tjosvold & Wisse, 2009). The first known source for this concept is Mary Parker Follett (Metcalf & Urwick, 1940/2013). Her work inspired generations of leadership scholars, although she was rarely acknowledged by them (Rusch, Gosetti, & Mohoric, 1991). In the leadership literature, Bennis and Nanus (2003) defined power as "the capacity to translate intention into reality and sustain it" (p. 16). Gardner (1990) understood it as "the capacity to bring about certain intended consequences in the behavior of others" (p. 55). Yukl (2009) described power as "the capacity to influence the attitudes and behavior of other people in the desired direction" (p. 218). From these examples, power as capacity is understood to mean having the power to affect an outcome, generally by a leader moving people in a desired direction.

If power is a capacity, it means that it is something that an individual learns how to express, and that one could also learn to express it in terms of each of the three locutions.

Inspired by Karlberg's (2005) unified schema of power (p. 10), the framework in Figure 3 presents a model for conceptualizing power as capacity. The model captures the three most common locutions of power presented in the literature and demonstrates how power as capacity can be manifest in multiple ways in addition to power as dominance. While not discussed as part of this inquiry, *balance of power* represents two adversarial sides holding equal power. As a result of this balance, neither party is able to dominate, potentially leading to stalemate, compromise, and frustrations (Karlberg, 2005). It is neither productive nor generative.

Power as Capacity

Constraining Relations		Capability: Individual or Relational	Mutualistic Relations	
power over		*power to*	*power with*	
dominance	ableness	cooperation		
Inequality	**Equality**	**Individual**	**Inequality**	**Equality**
Suppression	*Balance of power*	*Productive*	*Releasing capacity*	*Power sharing*
Win/lose	Lose/lose	Accomplish	Win/(win)	Win/win
Coercion	Stalemate	Resistance	Education	Synergy
Oppression	Compromise	Ability	Nurturance	Collaboration
Domination	Frustration	Potential	Assistance	Coordination

Figure 3. A unified framework of power. Adapted from "The power of discourse and the discourse of power: Pursuing peace through discourse intervention," by M. Karlberg, 2005, *International Journal of Peace Studies, 10*(1), 1-23. Adapted with permission.

Relational Power

The construction of power is as much the product of relational processes as it is of individual capacities. M. Gergen (1995) observed that within the social sciences, theories of power are generally entitative in nature. That is, they largely focus on leader cognition and capacities. The discourse on relational power resides within a comparably smaller community. However small, it is a no less important segment of the literature. From a social constructionist perspective, individual capacities do not develop in a void; they evolve through relational processes. That is, we develop our understanding of and capacities for power through our interactions with others.

Boulding (1990) posited that "the ability to communicate underlies all forms of power" (p. 110). In this sense, power emerges through dialogue. All parties participate in power's construction, whether through consent or constraint, and all personal conceptions are tied to those of the community (M. Gergen, 1995). A relational perspective offers the possibility of foregrounding processes and forces within social systems that are covert and/or invisible when viewed only from the perspective of the individual. As with collaborative leadership, a relational lens holds the possibility of opening new perspectives on power.

K. J. Gergen (1995) and Hosking (1995) are the two primary scholars who theorize power within a relational context. They noted that it is not otherwise discussed within the social constructionist literature. Both agreed that power is socially constructed between individuals and among groups through a process of social discourse where conversation represents the primary method of relating. It should be noted that other vehicles for learning such as observation and role modeling are equally important (Bandura, 1999). K. J. Gergen and Hosking both posited reasons for the lack of theorizing about power.

K. J. Gergen (1995) stated that power is "rhetorically red hot; it is suffused with the revolutionary energies of countless diatribes against inequality, oppression, and domination" (p. 29). He argued that organizational theorists would threaten their discipline by suggesting that organizations are replete with oppression and require fundamental change. A limitation of Gergen's argument is his dismissal of broader constructions of power beyond "power- over." Similar to Lukes (2005) and Wartenberg (1990), he confined his relational lens to the exposition of power as dominance and its concomitant oppression. Gergen assumed that interdependence requires shared constructions, and that interdependence can lead to oppression. This stance ignores the possibility that interdependence and a diversity of perspectives could coexist. In today's social worlds, the reality of the coexistence of difference and interdependence is evident in growing numbers of social communities. And, such coexistence may in fact become a necessity in the face of heightened complexity and the need for a diversity of perspectives to address the mounting challenges in our world.

Hosking (1995) suggested that the paucity of discourses about power within the relational literature results from it being hidden within the structures and language of organizations. She also challenged K. J. Gergen's (1995) stance about limiting the construction of power to dominance. She held that one of the values of a relational lens is, in fact, that alternative constructions of power can become visible. Hosking weakens her argument with two errors. First, she promoted a relational lens over an entitative one on the basis that entitative theorizing is individualistic, and therefore only constructions of dominance are possible within that frame. As was previously discussed in the exploration of power as capacity, this is not the case. As was noted, if power is a capacity one can learn to express multiple locutions. She also conflated power with hierarchy and knowledge, thereby cloaking power within these concepts. Hierarchy may modify or help to define power, but they are distinct concepts (Jaques, 1990).

Hosking (1995) further posited that only a constructionist-relational lens could offer a view of power in equal terms. However, Karlberg (2005) demonstrated otherwise with his entitative-relational model of power. When his model of power as capacity is mapped on an axis of equality-inequality, it becomes apparent that interrelationships do not have fixed points (see Figure 4). Rather, they are seen to be more or less equal or unequal and can shift and change along this axis. The same can be said for the adversarial-mutualistic axis. It should be noted that both K. J. Gergen's (1995) and Hosking's (1995) arguments were articulated at a time when the current theorizing discourses about collaborative forms of leadership were only just beginning.

However, in the intervening years they have not refuted or adjusted their respective stances with regards to power.

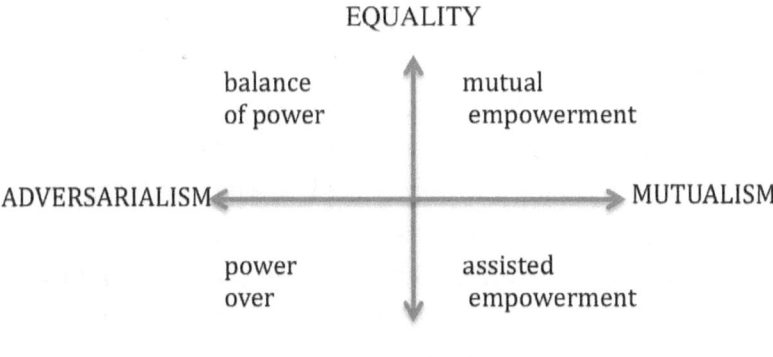

Figure 4. Relational and distributive dimensions of power. From "The power of discourse and the discourse of power: Pursuing peace through discourse intervention," by M. Karlberg, 2005, *International Journal of Peace Studies, 10*(1), 1-23.

The relational lens offers important value to the exploration of the construction of power. While this study is conducted largely within the frame of an entitative perspective, a relational lens can provide critique and expose covert processes—both positive and negative—that other perspectives cannot offer.

Power and Leadership

Having set the context through an overview of the broader power literature, the following offers a review of important considerations in any discussion of power and leadership. These are power and structure, and power and influence.

Power and Structure. An important issue in the study of power and leadership is the association of power to hierarchy as the two are frequently conflated. Shapiro (2003) observed that power theorists have tended to ignore the relationship between power and structure, and that the literature is "more suggestive than instructive" in this regard (p. 35). Despite this lack of theorizing, scholars have tended to view hierarchy as the assumed organizational structure, particularly where power is constructed as dominance.

While hierarchy tends to be associated with status and privilege, hierarchy itself is innocuous. As indicated earlier, it means a stratum of positions, ranked one upon the other where each level is subordinate to the one above. Leaders create hierarchies for the purpose of dealing with increasingly broader and more complex issues and organizations (Jaques, 1990). When leaders construct power as domination they tend to conflate power with hierarchy as it is thought to be essential for effective decision-making in such structures. However, hierarchies need not only be equated with domination (Jaques, 1990). Such conceptualizing overlooks the potential dynamics that can emerge when power is constructed in mutualistic terms.

Harkening back to Karlberg's (2005) schema of power, one of the goals of mutualistic power is to develop the capacity of followers such that their capacities will be more closely aligned to those of the leader. As Karlberg suggested in his model of relational and distributive dimensions of power (see Figure 4), when this occurs the possibility that leaders and followers can mutually empower one another also emerges. Relational equality becomes possible in decision-making. Follett's (Metcalf & Urwick, 1940/2013) law of the situation also becomes possible. Follett believed that the person most qualified in a given situation would take a leadership role for the issue at hand. It is equally conceivable that leaders can become followers in that instance.

When mutualism is introduced as an important expression of power within a group or organization the purpose of hierarchy does not necessarily change. It continues to aid in addressing the leader's larger scope of responsibility and higher levels of complexity. However, hierarchy may serve as a barrier to mutualism when it is conflated with domination, privilege, or status. Leaders who promote mutualism may also promote relational equality, particularly in terms of consensus building and decision-making, as a counter measure to the power gap created by dominance. Relational equality means that all members of the group relate as equals; each person's perspective is viewed as equal to all others.

When relational equality is promoted leaders are combining hierarchy with heterarchy. Stark (2001) explained that the hallmarks of heterarchical structures are distributed intelligence and coordination across diverse perspectives. While he did not define distributed intelligence, it is a term adopted from network theory to explain the distribution of information and decision- making across a networked structure characterized by relational equality of units and subunits. Stark posited that such organizational diversity of structure promotes adaptability, and adaptability is understood to be an important capacity in the face of rising complexity. Uhl-Bien et al. (2007) made similar assertions in their exploration of what they term complexity leadership. In light of these perspectives, it is possible to predict that when hierarchical and heterarchical structures coexist, mutualistic power will become the leader's preferred construction.

Power and Influence. Another topic of importance within the leadership and power literature is the relationship of power and influence. Despite their distinct definitions, these terms are frequently treated as synonymous in the literature (Göhler, 2009). For example, Dahl (1957) launched his essay on the concept of power by explaining that he would use these terms interchangeably, acknowledging that to do so is reflective of Western vernacular. Influence is generally treated in the same manner as Weber interpreted power, suggesting that there is an individual actor exercising dominance over another in order to exert one's will. Thus, the conflation of power and influence has further served to reinforce the notion of power as dominance, particularly as it is applied within the leadership literature.

Agency and Communion

The third literature of importance to this study is agency and communion. Agency and communion are terms coined by Bakan (1966) to represent two basic motivations that inform human behavior and symbolize fundamental challenges of the human condition (Abele & Wojciszke, 2013; De Dreu & Nauta, 2009; McAdams, Hoffman, Mansfield, & Day, 1996; Ybarra et al., 2008). However, the concepts that underpin agency and communion precede Bakan's work. For example, Wiggins (1991) traced their lineage back as far as Confucius. Since Bakan (1966) published *The Duality of Human Existence*, multiple disciplines have taken up the study of these "big two" dimensions (Abele & Wojciszke, 2013; Bruckmüller & Abele, 2013). In fact, Paulhus and Trapnell (2008) considered agency and communion to be "the single most powerful framework for organizing the field of human personality" (p. 496).

Agency animates achievement behaviors such as ambition, competence, and dominance.

It promotes self-expression, assertiveness, and self-protection. It is commonly associated with power and is given preeminent status in Western culture (Bakan, 1966; Diehl, Owen, & Youngblade, 2004; Nisbett, 2003). As such, agency is frequently equated with maturity and human flourishing. Kegan (1994) explained how this is a false equation and that agency is a stylistic preference, while maturity is a structural distinction. This issue will be pursued further below. Here, it is important to note that agency is also associated with alienation and with much of what ails humanity today (Bakan, 1966; Csikszentmihalyi, 1993; Guisinger & Blatt, 1994). On the other hand, communal desires are understood to promote relationship maintenance behaviors such as cooperativeness, nurturance, and emphasizing others (Abele & Wojciszke, 2007; Ybarra et al., 2008).

How to balance agency and communion has become an important question in the psychology literature. Most scholars acknowledge that both are equally important (Bauer & McAdams, 2004; Diehl et al., 2004; Eagly & Carli, 2007; Frimer, Walker, Lee, Riches, & Dunlop, 2012). Increasingly, scholars are also exploring this question in the context of leadership

(Eagly & Carli, 2007; Edmondson, 2012; Gino, 2013). The study of traditional approaches to leadership has revealed the limitations of hierarchical models that tend to overemphasize agency to the exclusion of the communal aspects of human nature (Gronn, 2008). Today, leaders need the agility to lead both hierarchically and heterarchically, where heterarchy is more closely associated with communal behaviors than is hierarchy. Leaders also require the capacity to discern when one or the other best meets the needs of the current context. This may require the leader to balance agency and communion.

Two concepts pivotal to our understanding of how to balance agency and communion are structure and style (Hatcher, 1982; Kegan, 1994). They represent our primary ways of knowing, or how we organize our experiences. Structural theories assume that we construct our reality by being active agents in giving form and consistency to our experiences, and that we may also progress through increasing levels of capacity to make sense of these experiences. Structural theories are referred to as subject-object theories. At each progressive stage of development, humans are thought to develop the capacity to objectify that which they were subject to or guided by in their previous stage. As our capacities increase, so too does our ability to think in more complex ways (Csikszentmihalyi, 1993; Kegan, 1994). While stylistic theories are also constructivist, they address our preferences for, or our orientation to, making meaning of our experiences.

Kegan (1994) noted that while both structure and style are important for growth, they are frequently conflated in the literature. Although related, they are in fact distinct concepts. Style does not increase capacity, but it can transform how capacities are expressed as a person progresses through stages of development (Kegan, 1994). In particular, the stylistic motivations of agency and communion are commonly mistaken for the structural developmental processes of differentiation and integration. Whereas agency and communion speak to how one might choose to self-authorize, differentiation means to be separate or independent in one's behavior. A desire for independence (style) or to express one's agency is not the same as having the ability to think for oneself (structure). And being communal or relational is not the same as being integrated.

Being relational is about connection with others. Integration represents the process of consolidating growth attained while moving through a process of differentiation. Thus, a person can be both relational *and* differentiated or independent *and* integrated.

Kegan (1994) observed that stylistic preferences such as agency and communion would be manifest at all stages of development. As an individual progresses through more advanced stages the manner in which they manifest these behaviors may change as a result of increased maturity and objectivity. When individuals are functioning at more advanced stages of development, they would have also developed the capacity to be aware of their stylistic options and to be increasingly more proactive in their responses. They would be able to exercise choice and discretion at the same time (Hatcher, 1982; Kegan, 1994). Studies of people who are seen to be moral exemplars suggest that such individuals exercise clear choices for their behavior (Frimer, Walker, Dunlop, Lee, & Riches, 2011). They also tend to apply their agency in a communal manner. That is, they employ agency in service to others. Frimer et al. called this "enlightened self-interest" (p. 161). Kegan referred to this as a "jointly structural and stylistic apprehension of the self and its development" (p. 229). A corollary of this balancing would be to choose how one uses power. Leaders who engage in enlightened self-interest would be expected to prefer mutualistic expressions of power.

Constructivism

Constructivism is the fourth and final literature of importance to this study. Its importance resides in the guidance it provides for understanding why there are two distinct ways of understanding the phenomena of leadership and power, and how both entitative and relational ways of knowing can be complementary to one another. This inquiry is concerned with two theories of constructivism: cognitive (individual/entitative) and social constructionist (collective/relational). While social constructionism will be explored in Chapter 3 in terms of how it influences methodology, this discussion considers how cognitive and social constructionist theories help to clarify collaborative leaders' construction of or meaning making about power.

Cognitive Theory

The cognitive theory that resonates best with this study is Kegan's (1982, 1994) constructive-developmental theory. It is founded on a teleological paradigm that assumes individuals develop the capacity for progressively more complex ways of thinking about themselves and others (Bauer & McAdams, 2004). This capacity is represented by discrete stages of development where each successive stage builds upon the previous one. New capacities transcend the skills, behaviors, and worldviews that have preceded them. As cognitive structures develop, individuals are able to think and respond in increasingly more complex ways.

Kegan's (1982, 1994) work is rooted in the constructivist theories of Swiss psychologist and epistemologist Jean Piaget, who was concerned with how individuals mentally organize the world. Constructivism explores internal processes in which the individual is an active participant in meaning making (Greeno et al., 1996; C. C. Liu & I Ju, 2010). Earlier versions of constructivism argued that meaning making is the product of an interaction between individual thoughts and experiences. More recent developments acknowledge the role that social and cultural influences also play on individual thinking (Sjøberg, 2010).

Social Constructionist Theory

Social constructionism accentuates the role of social discourse and action (Krebs, 2004).

The development of this theory was influenced by the work of Russian psychologist Lev Vygotsky. It considers meaning making as a dynamic process of co-construction among participants who are party to a given interaction. Knowledge is distributed and the act of construction is the product of relationships and not the possession of individuals (Dachler & Hosking, 1995). Gergen (2009) stated, "it is through coordinated action—not individual minds— that meaning originates" (p. 397). Truth claims are evaluated against the effects of social, cultural, and ethical influences on discourse and action (Krebs, 2004). Truth will therefore vary, dependent upon context. Construction is not a one-time event. It is understood to be an "ongoing process of relating" (Dachler & Hosking, 1995, p. 3).

Cognitive meaning-making processes are understood to be universal; that is, they apply to everyone, whereas those of social constructionism are embedded in the immediate sociocultural context. Cognitive theories present development as an individual process where development is understood to precede growth. Within social constructionism, development is the product of social engagement where interaction precedes and promotes development.

Fairhurst and Grant (2010) noted that the fundamental distinction between these two theories is that cognitive theories represent the construction of social reality—an individual endeavor— while relational approaches represent the social construction of reality—a collective endeavor.

As discussed earlier, the proposed study investigates both individual (entitative) and interactive (relational) ways that leaders construct power. The objective is to gain a multi-dimensional perspective. Cognitive theories offer the possibility of shedding light on how individual leaders construct power. Social constructionist theories offer a window onto construction through coordinated action. While the primary focus of this study is on the individual leaders, relational aspects are also of importance if one is to secure a more holistic perspective on the construction of a concept.

Each of these theories represents a distinctive worldview and is considered to be incommensurate with one another. Each asks questions based on differing assumptions about what constitutes knowledge. However, it is possible to view them as complementary in that they both illumine some aspect of how humans learn. The need to think in complementary or both/and terms becomes paramount in highly complex circumstances.

From an organizational perspective, the capacities of individual leaders have been outdistanced by the rising complexity of modern life and its concomitant challenges. Yet organizational research lags in its efforts to explore new ways of addressing such concerns (Uhl- Bien & Ospina, 2012). Facing these challenges requires distributed knowledge and relational solutions. These, in turn, demand of leaders to choose broader conceptions of power. The application of social constructionist theories to leadership studies is relatively new and promising, as is the application of multiple methodologies. They both offer the potential to generate new insights about leadership and power that may aid in defining "the future direction of the field" (Uhl-Bien & Ospina, 2012, p. xxii).

Entitative and Relational Lenses

The decision to emphasize an entitative lens over a relational one as the primary focus of this study is important to clarify. To do so is not to promote one perspective over another. Both offer significant value. The issue is in part methodological. To employ a relational lens would require observation of group processes and conversations over an extended period of time. This presents logistical challenges for both the researcher and the organizations under study, particularly when the organization members are globally dispersed. Observation can also promote discomfort and potential "performance anxiety" for those under observation, thereby altering natural responses.

There is also an ontological reason for this choice. K. J. Gergen (1995) posited that humans "do not commence life as single, unitary or self-contained monads but gain their very capacity to exist in such apparent states (what we call states of individual identity) by virtue of their relatedness" (p. 36). Hatcher (1982) was in agreement with Gergen that relationships and environment play a significant role in human development. However, he also observed that people have inherited innate traits that are unique to them. These traits distinguish one person from another. In turn, individuals respond in their own way to the influences of relationships and the environment.

Hatcher's (1982) perspective aligns with Kegan's (1994) constructive-developmental theory. People who (cognitively) construct the world in more advanced ways will tend to think in a more critical manner. Thus, they have the capacity to rise above the dominant conversation and introduce new and revised constructions into the general discourse. The general discourse, in turn, serves to shape and define each of us. It is possible that leaders who construct power in new and different ways are doing so from more advanced stages of development. Thus, focusing on an entitative lens can reveal insights about how leaders construct power in ways that a relational one cannot.

Leadership and Power

The following section integrates the collaborative leadership and power literatures in order to demonstrate the gap that currently exists between them. As indicated earlier, leadership and power have been considered by many to be synonymous. Gardner (1990) observed that while leadership and power are not the same, they "interweave at many points" (p. 55). He believed that the central concerns at their synapse were how leaders acquire power and how they wield it. Gronn (2008) viewed them to have "close conceptual links" (p. 142). And Nye (2010) stated, "one cannot lead without power" (p. 306).

How leaders think about and use power will impact how they practice leadership and will influence how power emerges within the system. From this perspective, power can be said to represent the nucleus of leadership. However, these are two distinct concepts and they need to be considered separately. To conflate leadership and power cloaks from view the multiple conceptions of power that are possible.

Shamir (2012) posited that a differentiation of influence, and therefore power, represents the fundamental nature of leadership. His argument represents an example of the limitations created by such a conflation. He held to the view that power is a form of dominance and thus can be wielded by only one party at a time. Shamir stated,

> For a phenomenon to be called *leadership*, we have to be able to identify certain actors who, at least in a certain situation and during a specified period of time, exert more influence than others on the group or the process. (p. 487) In other words, leadership is a solo act even if that act can shift to different people.

Inequality of influence is linked directly to power differentials. That is, leadership is constituted by one person holding a power differential and therefore having a greater possibility of influencing others. Shamir (2012) maintained that the concept of asymmetric influence by single actors must be retained if the construct of leadership is to remain useful. This position would seem to be accurate if power is constructed only as a form of dominance. As discussed earlier, this is the prevailing view of the relationship between leadership and power.

At the same time, power has tended to be viewed as something not to be trusted (Bennis, 2003; Kanter, 1994; Pfeffer, 1992; Torbert, 1991). Most leadership studies avoid the topic entirely (Bennis & Nanus, 2003). Kanter (1994) underlined this point when she referred to power as "America's last dirty word" (p. 1). Torbert (1991) reinforced this point of view when he commented that power is used primarily to dominate, and, as such, is "inherently disintegrative, hierarchical, uninquiring, and corrupting" (p. 2). Pfeffer (1992) believed that our disdain for power stems primarily from the fact that it can be wielded for both good and evil, and that we are not schooled in the effective use of power. Fletcher (2004) contended that part of the issue lies at the heart of how we conceptualize power. She believed that we tend to view it in gendered terms, where adversarial competitive manifestations are considered as having power-over and tend to be labelled masculine. Meanwhile, non-adversarial, mutualistic expressions categorized as power-with tend to be viewed as feminine. As masculinity and work are typically conflated adversarial power has been exalted and feminine power devalued.

Prescribed frameworks reinforce this negative perception of power, indicating that a top- down model employing competitive, constraining power is the norm. For example, Pfeffer (1992) believed that leaders need an "understanding that to get things done, you need power— more power than those whose opposition you must overcome—and thus it is imperative to understand where power comes from and how these sources of power can be developed" (p. 46). As indicated earlier, this prevalent point of view is sustained in part by the dominant discourse in society that tends to view power in competitive and conflictual terms (Karlberg, 2005). The goal is one of winning or having outcomes align with one's personal intentions (Kellerman, 2012).

Similar to the larger corpus of leadership literature, where power is addressed in the collaborative leadership literature, it generally tends to be viewed as a possession of the leader. For example, Denis et al. (2012) noted that when leadership is pooled at the top, consideration is given mainly to how power is shared among coleaders. The senior leader is understood to hold power, but must wrestle with how it is utilized with others who are considered equal. In leader- follower arrangements the focus tends to be on empowerment, where the underlying concept is one of the powerful sharing with the powerless (Fletcher & Käufer, 2003). Empowerment is understood to represent the gifting of power (Denis et al., 2012).

Both of these discussions suggest that power is a

possession. Such a stance presents a significant challenge for widespread adoption of collaborative leadership, at least in the near term. As Fletcher and Käufer (2003) noted, when power is seen as something that can be owned it becomes incumbent upon those in positions of power to drive its distribution. When there is no clear motivation to do so sharing is less likely. Leaders also remain accountable for group meaning making in terms of how members "understand themselves, their work, and others engaged in that work" (Friedrich et al., 2009, p. 940). So long as those at the highest levels of organizations maintain this meaning making the realization of the full potential for collaboration and mutualism will be thwarted.

As was argued in the power literature review, power is more realistically thought of as capacity rather than as a possession. Individuals must develop their ability to access and utilize power. When the leader's role shifts from gifting power to one of drawing out or releasing capacity there is no loss of power to the leader. This becomes a win-win-win proposition for the leaders, followers, and the organization. The more capacity each person has the more potential the organization will have.

Broader constructions of power beyond the dominant paradigm of dominance are needed. Trist (1977) advised almost 40 years ago that such a shift must take place if societies and organizations are to be equipped to address the growing complexity and turbulence in the world. Many scholars who assume this stance endorse mutualistic forms of power. For example, Torbert (1991) employed the term non-adversarial power that he views as "inherently integrative, mutual, inquiring and ethical" (p. 2). Kanter (1994) considered mutualistic power to be productive, positing that it provides greater returns for the organization. Employing an economic model, she explained that nations accrue greater returns in their productive capacity when they invest in their skill base. Mutualistic expressions of power would ultimately increase the leader's power rather than diminish it, to the overall benefit of the organization.

At a macro level, there is a growing understanding that organizations need to make this shift in thinking (Fletcher, 2004; Kanter, 1994). This is true in part because an increasingly important way that individual success in organizations is measured is in terms of how well people can work with and through others (Kanter, 1994; Pfeffer, 1992). Nye (2010) confirmed this shift when he observed that effective leaders do confine their use of power. He also stated that recent studies indicate adolescents may show a preference for mutualistic power, suggesting that for mutualistic power to become the dominant paradigm, a generational change may be required.

However this shift occurs, until the dominant leadership discourse evolves to include more stories about broader forms of power and collaborative approaches to leadership, the prevailing worldview will most likely remain entrenched in the traditional paradigm where unequal power is the norm (Fletcher, 2004).

While there are gaps within and across various collaborative leadership theories (Bolden, 2011; Denis et al., 2012; Fitzsimons et al., 2011; Thorpe et al., 2011), from the perspective of this study the gap of greatest interest is in the treatment of power (Denis et al., 2012; Gronn, 2008). Because leadership and power are so closely aligned, theorizing will remain incomplete until this gap is filled. Also, as Fletcher (2004) observed, such an exploration is essential to realizing the transformative potential of collaborative leadership theories. Collaborative leadership represents devolution of power from the individual heroic leader to followers within the organization in a distributed configuration. For this reason, it is logical to assume that collaborative leaders will differ from more traditional leaders in terms of how they construct power.

Evidence of this perspective exists from some of the earliest writings about collaborative leadership and continues into the present. Follett (Metcalf & Urwick, 1940/2013), who produced the majority of her work in the 1920s, proposed that instead of any role or person having power over another, power could be developed jointly. She named this "co-active, not a coercive power" (p. 101) as in power-with, envisioning it as a reachable goal between management and workers. Follett challenged the notion that power is something that a leader is able to delegate.

She viewed power as a capacity and therefore as something that must be drawn out of a person rather than something that can be deposited or distributed (Youngs, 2009). Follett said,

> I do not think that power can be delegated because I believe that genuine power is capacity. To confer power on the workers may be an empty gesture. The main problem of the workers is by no means how much control they can wrest from capital or management, often as we hear that stated; that would be a merely nominal authority and would slip quickly from their grasp. Their problem is how much power they can themselves grow. The matter of workers' control which is so often thought of as a matter of how much the managers will be willing to give up, is really as much a matter for the workers, how much will they be able to assume; where the managers come in is that they should give the workers a chance to grow capacity or power for themselves. (Graham, 2003, p. 111)

Leadership theorists such as Peter F. Drucker and Rosabeth Moss Kanter acknowledged the inspiration they took from Follet's work (Graham, 2003). Rusch et al. (1991)

posited that Follett equally provided inspiration for James McGregor Burns' (1978) landmark publication *Leadership*. In their comparison of these two authors, Rusch et al. found a number of direct parallels. There is one of particular note for this study. Burns is celebrated for his concept of transforming leadership. He wrote that transforming leadership emphasizes leaders collaborating with followers to identify needed change, create a vision to guide the change, and to execute the change in tandem (*Transformational leadership*, n.d.). He envisioned that the transforming leader "taps the needs and raises the aspirations and helps shape the values—and hence mobilizes the potential—of followers" (Burns, 1978, p. 455). Rusch et al. observed that Follet had already employed the concept of transforming leadership. Follet wrote, "When leadership rises to genius it has the power of transforming, of transforming experience into power. And that is what experience is for, to be made into power" (Graham, 2003, p. 169). It is interesting to note that Burn's work provided the inspiration for a number of authors who were subsequently exalted as thought leaders. Among them are Warren Bennis, Burt Nanus, Thomas Peters, and Robert Waterman.

Contemporary authors such as Kouzes and Posner (1987/2002) and Fletcher and Käufer (2003) also explore the concept of mutualistic power. Kouzes and Posner propose that power sharing between leaders and followers produces significant benefits for both individuals and the organization. Individuals develop their competence and confidence, gain a sense of self- leadership, and assume accountability. As individuals are strengthened, so too is the organization.

Fletcher and Käufer (2003) theorize about shared leadership based on Scharmer's (2000) model of four phases of learning conversations. They propose that generative dialogue equates to shared leadership (see Figure 5). Generative dialogue can emerge in the presence of power sharing. Collectives fully engage with one another and co-lead themselves. Shared understanding results from mutuality, learning, and co-created solutions. The entire system is focused on the common good. Power dynamics become fluid, where expertise is "continually being shifted and redefined to include other perspectives (p. 40).

From these examples, it becomes clear that discussions of power are central to our understanding of collaborative leadership and that the gap in the literature between these two concepts are important areas of research if the concept of collaborative leadership is to be advanced and more broadly adopted.

Summary

The prominent discourse about power in Western cultures is of dominance (Gordon, 2008; Karlberg, 2005; Seers et al., 2003). Dominance has been equated with agency, and agency in Western cultures is associated with power (Bakan, 1966). Leadership is understood to be synonymous with status, privilege, and hierarchy. This conflation, particularly of hierarchy and power, has masked more human-centered aspects of leadership and broader possibilities for how we might define power, especially in terms of mutualistic expressions.

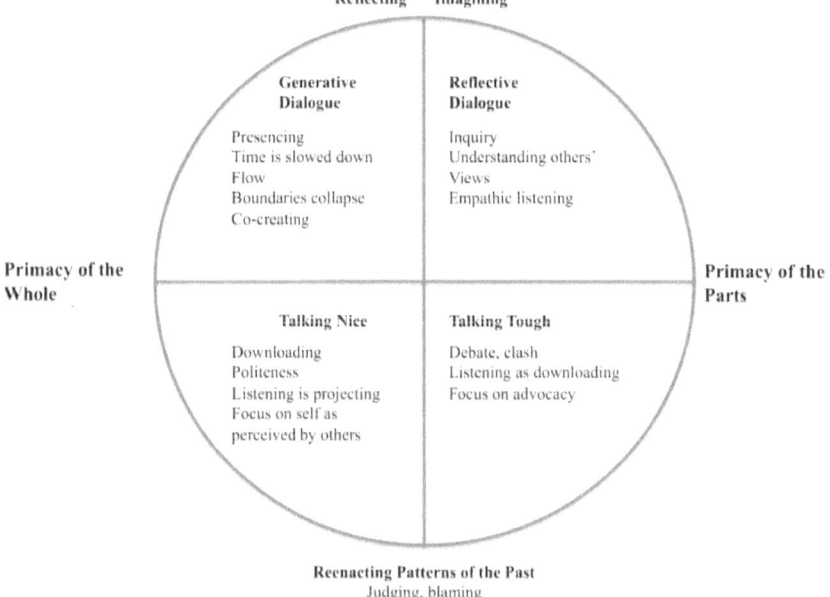

Figure 5. Dialogue: four phases of learning conversations. Adapted from Scharmer (2000) and replicated from Fletcher and Käufer (2003).

Maintaining notions of asymmetric power as the singular way to construct power in leadership is a lose-lose proposition for everyone. As our social worlds become increasingly complex, leaders and followers need to engage in new ways. Leaders need to engage followers in consultations and decision-making and followers need to feel safe to fully express themselves and develop their potential. Power as dominance constrains both of these actions.

Because leadership and power are so tightly fused, it is essential that new and broader constructions of power be explored if theory is to be advanced. Such constructions are emerging. A review of the power literature indicates that dominance is but one form of power. Power as ableness or power-to and as mutualism or power-with are equally valid and important constructs. If we embrace these broader constructions of power, it will become possible to consider new relationships between leadership and power beyond dominance.

Within the context of collaborative leadership as it is expressed at this time, leaders continue to hold ultimate responsibility. They have the opportunity to exercise power as an expression of both dominance and mutualism. However, their goal is to maximize coordinated decision-making and action. Thus, one would expect collaborative leaders to avoid or minimize exercising power over others even though it is always at their disposal. One would also expect collaborative leaders to hold a preference for employing power with others to the fullest extent possible. These are matters of choice.

Agency and communion represent two primary motivations of human behavior. Agency is understood to represent domination and is associated with power. Communality represents relational behaviors such as cooperation and other-centeredness. How one employs these modalities is a matter of choice. Western cultures tend to privilege agency over communion or the individual over the collective. This preference influences social discourse and therefore how central concepts such as leadership and power are both theorized and manifested.

In the contemporary leadership discourse, two lenses have emerged as important ways to study leadership. The entitative and the relational lenses offer the possibility of exploring leadership in distinct but complementary ways. They are distinct to the extent that they are founded on and informed by different theories of what constitutes reality and what constitutes knowledge. They are also complementary because both can provide insights about the same phenomenon. While collaborative approaches to leadership have been explored through each of these lenses, few studies from either lens have given consideration to the question of power.

To be fully constituted, a phenomenon such as power requires both thought and action. Constructivist theory offers a framework for exploring power through both an entitative and a relational lens. The entitative lens considers what leaders are thinking about power and the relational one looks at the dynamics of power within a system.

Research Question

This review of the literature reveals a gap in the study of collaborative leadership and power. Because power is intrinsic to leadership, such a study is essential. The research question that guides this study asks, how do leaders who are identified as collaborative construct power? The participants and organizations in this study consciously practice a collaborative style of leadership. Third parties have identified them as collaborative in their approach to leadership.

In an effort to bring clarity to this study, I have employed the term *collaborative leadership* going forward, unless specific literatures are under discussion. There are several important reasons for making this choice. First, none of the theories within this field fully represent all that is emerging in practice (Davis, 2013). The current study is further evidence of this, as will be discussed in Chapter 5. Secondly, collaborative leadership is a term that leaders choose to describe their practice (Davis, 2013). This fact was also confirmed during the data gathering for this study. Finally, the etymology of the word *collaborate* denotes colaboring, which is reflective of what the leaders in this study are endeavoring to do across their organizations. It also aligns with an emerging discourse in society about collaboration that is reflected in everything from political to consumer consumption movements.

CHAPTER THREE

METHODOLOGY

Chapter 3 outlines the research design for this study. A research design aligns the facets of the inquiry, from the epistemological framework and theoretical perspective to the methodology and methods (Creswell, 2013; Crotty, 1998). Each facet of this study is described.

The epistemological framework is based on Smith and Karlberg's (2009) *consultative epistemology.* This framework explains how two distinct worldviews can be bridged to provide complementary perspectives about a given phenomenon. Given this duality, it follows that two theoretical perspectives and two methodologies would inform the study design. The theoretical perspectives applied here are postpositivism and interpretivism, and the two methodologies are phenomenology and ethnography. The methods for data collection are semistructured qualitative interviews, observation of group interaction, and analysis of documentation pertaining to organizational systems and structures. Thematic analysis was employed for all three types of the collected data. However, there are distinctions in the approach across the data sources. For the interview data, the interest was specifically in leaders' thoughts about power. For the group observations and systems and structures, the search was for how power manifests in the system. Individual actions shift to the background and the focus turns to what is occurring in the system. The following sections outline each of these facets of the research design and provide further details on the methods used.

Epistemological Framework

Smith and Karlberg's (2009) consultative epistemology holds that there is an objective reality; however, our individual ability to access it is limited and fallible. Gaining as broad an understanding as possible requires multiple and diverse points of view. Because each person may have some access to truth, it is possible to gain a wider perspective when we collaborate.

An obvious question arises as to how we can know that a true approximation of reality has been attained. Smith and Karlberg (2009) explained that phenomena are more or less tangible and therefore more or less accessible or able to be socially constructed. Highly tangible phenomena such as pain are less likely to be subject to social construction, as are highly intangible phenomena such as dreams. Phenomena that claim a middle ground are more likely candidates. Over time, approximation to objective reality becomes recognizable. The example Smith and Karlberg offered was the growing body of knowledge associated with health and healing. Over time, medical science learns what approaches are best applied to restore a patient's health. The objective truth in this example is that a person's health can be restored. How the truth is uncovered is the project of social construction. We socially construct healing until reality has been approximated. In this case, reality is that the patient is healed.

Smith and Karlberg (2009) also called our attention to an important corollary of the principles of consultative epistemology. While an objective reality is understood to exist, some paradigms may be better suited to accessing particular aspects of it than others. From a research perspective, employing multiple perspectives becomes critical until we have solid evidence about which ones are most suited to an inquiry. For example, this could mean gathering evidence from both an entitative and a relational perspective.

This study explored how leaders construct power from both an entitative and a relational perspective. The entitative lens is traditionally employed for leadership studies. Through it, researchers consider individual attributes and/or perspectives. Explanatory forces are considered to be the possession of the individual or entity (Dachler & Hosking, 1995). For example, power is seen as the possession and prerogative of a leader. Relationships are considered in subject- object terms from the perspective of the entity. Leaders are subjects and those over whom they apply power—typically referred to as followers—are objects. As a result, the leader/follower relationship is rarely theorized within the leadership literature (Dachler & Hosking, 1995).

However, Fitzsimons et al. (2011) noted the potential weaknesses of solely employing the entitative lens in a study of leadership. In this paradigm, precedence is given to cognitive processes, thereby minimizing the role of other constituent contributors, such as followers, or context such as organizational systems. Applying a second lens—a relational one—not only broadens our understanding of phenomena such as power, but also reveals the interactive dynamics that play an important role in fully constituting phenomena in the context of leadership.

A relational lens is rooted in social constructionist epistemology. It shifts the emphasis to the collective where knowledge is distributed and socially constructed. Meaning derives from "interwoven narratives recounted within a cultural community" (Dachler & Hosking, 1995, p. 3). A relational perspective considers subject and object to be partners in knowledge generation. Knowing is relative to and occurs within a context. It is understood to be an ongoing, dynamic, and ever-changing process, rather than an event. Dachler and Hosking offered the example of waving wildly. This action has no inherent meaning unto itself. Nothing has meaning until it has been constructed, and the ascribed meaning will be embedded within a historically situated context. While individuals may perform the waving, they learn to do so within a cultural context. In other words, there are no universal truths.

Theoretical Perspective

The next stage in Crotty's (1998) schema is to make explicit one's theoretical perspective. Two perspectives inform this research study: postpositivism and interpretivism. A more holistic understanding of the construction of power can be achieved by exploring processes that are individual/cognitive (postpositivist) and relational/intersubjective (interpretivist) in nature.

Postpositivism

In leadership studies, researchers who conduct inquiries of individuals or entities frequently take a postpositivist stance. Postpositivists recognize that research is fallible and that researchers bring a subjective perspective to their work. They also acknowledge that within these varying perspectives, no one interpretation may be correct and that "belief in reality and in truth is not undermined by epistemological uncertainty about which account of reality is warranted" (Phillips & Burbules,

2000, p. 77). Governed by this perspective, researchers must continue to generate warrantable claims produced through rigorous methods and develop sufficient evidence in support of their claims to demonstrate as far as possible that these claims reflect truth. They must also investigate threats to the validity of their assertions by paying attention to disconfirming evidence (Phillips & Burbules, 2000).

Interpretivism

As the name implies, interpretivism engages the researcher in the interpretation of study elements. As with postpositivism, it emerged in response to the positivist stance (Crotty, 1998). As this perspective evolves, multiple schools or cultures of inquiry continue to develop (Bentz & Shapiro, 1998). However, most reflect similar assumptions. The primary ones are that reality is socially constructed, that we cannot separate ourselves from what we know, and that truth is negotiated through interaction. Research findings are not discovered. Rather, the researcher and the study participants cocreate them. All knowledge is contextual and open to dialogue.

Interpretivism shares with postpositivism the view that multiple perspectives are important and that researchers bring their personal values to any interpretation. However, their rationale for these views is different. From a postpositivist stance, the external world is knowable by the individual. However, each person can achieve only partial understanding. The interpretivist is committed to understanding the world as it is experienced, rather than explaining what exists (Burrell & Morgan, 1979). Reality is co-constructed in the collective, and the focus of research is the process by which this reality is co-constructed (Morgan & Smircich, 1980).

Interpretivism is also concerned with what is specific

and unique to a situation. Knowledge is understood to be relative. That is, it is bounded by time, context, and culture ("Interpretivism," 2014). The social world is thus "an emergent social process which is created by the individuals concerned" (Burrell & Morgan, 1979, p. 28). The focus of research shifts from the individual to the collective and to what is taking place within the collective rather than what any one individual is thinking or doing.

Methodology

According to Crotty's (1998) schema, one's choice of methodology should unite the study's theoretical perspective and methods employed. It will thereby indirectly align with the researcher's epistemological perspective. Methodologies represent "the strategy, plan or action, process or design" (Crotty, 1998, p. 3) of the study. As previously indicated, both postpositivist and interpretivist perspectives inform this study. To align with these theoretical perspectives, two distinct methodologies of phenomenology and ethnography have been employed.

Phenomenology

When approached from the theories of Edmund Husserl and Maurice Merleau-Ponty, phenomenology is in alignment with the theoretical assumptions of postpositivism (Clark, 1998; Creswell, 2013; Crotty, 1998; Moustakas, 1994; Rachler & Robinson, 2002). The postpositivist stance applies to the entitative or individual aspects of this study. It was employed here to explore how leaders think about the construction of power.

The link between postpositivism and phenomenology lies in the recognition of an objective reality, where the perceiver (subject) is separate from the perceived (object). Phenomenology seeks to understand phenomena as they are, rather than how they are received into our consciousness. The researcher is invited to engage directly with the *lived experience* of how participants make sense of a given phenomenon (Creswell, 2013). This requires that researchers set aside or "bracket" received understanding from their own surrounding context and culture in order that they might engage directly with phenomena under study without the influence of pre-existing interpretations. The goal of an inquiry is to uncover the "universal essence" of phenomena (Creswell, 2013, p. 76). This is achieved by exploring the common meaning across a group of people.

Moustakas's (1994) approach to phenomenology informs the research design for the entitative aspect of this study. It is applied to data gathering through qualitative interviews and also informs the interview protocol development and execution. Thematic analysis of the results is guided by both Moustakas (1994) and Richards (2009). Moustakas's approach was selected because he has integrated the leading theories on phenomenological research and presented them in an easily followed, step-by-step framework.

Ethnography

Smith and Karlberg (2009) posited that the space between the extremes of phenomena— those that are highly tangible and those that are least tangible—is the space where we socially construct our reality. This is the place where subject and object become one, and where descriptions of reality cannot be separated from the situated and historical standpoint of the observer. This is a space where ethnography can serve as a useful research tool.

Ethnography is an approach to research traditionally employed by anthropologists to offer an account of a situation. The researcher offers a third-person point of view, reporting facts and reserving judgment (Creswell, 2013). Data are gathered through detailed and descriptive field notes. Generally, the researcher spends an extended period of time observing a group within a shared culture. Although I was unable to observe the groups over an extended time period, I spent over 25 hours conducting interviews with members of the two organizations in this study, extensively explored organizational documentation, and observed meetings for several hours. All of these activities took place over a three-month period. Thus, the cultures of these organizations are not unfamiliar to me, and the data I was able to gather is robust.

Van Maanen (1988) described ethnography as "the peculiar practice of representing the social reality of others through the analysis of one's own experience in the world of these others" (p. xiii). The researcher analyzes the data in search of patterns of activity within the observed data (Van Maanen, 1979) and cataloging this activity as emergent themes. Ultimately, the researcher interprets the themes to generalize how the group works (Creswell, 2003). In this study, I applied an ethnographic lens to describe how power manifests within the two organizations under analysis.

Methods

Methods represent a reasoned set of tasks or specific steps one takes to fulfill the study design (Bentz & Shapiro, 1998). They connect to the chosen methodology and must be able to answer the research question that has been posed. Qualitative approaches are typically applied in the study of the common experience of a given phenomenon by a group of individuals (Creswell, 2013). In the case of this study, the common phenomenon is power. Conger believed that qualitative methodologies are responsible for paradigm shifts in our thinking, referring to the concept introduced by Kuhn (1962/1996).

This study represents fertile ground for a shift in paradigms about how leaders think about and use power. Creswell (2013) suggested three criteria for selecting qualitative methodologies: a) limited research has been conducted on the phenomenon or concept; b) the research is exploratory and therefore important variables are not known; c) the topic is new. As indicated through the literature review, the present inquiry meets all of these criteria.

The following discussion outlines the approaches used in this study for population sampling, the sample size, data collection, and data analysis. It also includes a review of the pilot study, a review of the actions taken to protect human subjects, and a discussion of the trustworthiness of the study findings. As a reminder, this study explores the construction of power by leaders who have been identified as collaborative in their approach. It does so from more than one perspective by gathering and evaluating data using multiple approaches. All of the methods employed in this study are qualitative in nature. They are purposive sampling, semistructured interviews, document analysis, participant observation, and thematic analysis.

Population Sampling

Neuman (1994) explained that sampling in social research typically applies to quantitative studies. Sampling means to "draw a sample from a larger pool of cases . . . in a population" (p. 195). However, there are instances where sampling becomes an important consideration in qualitative studies. This study explored a specific population of leaders. Identifying such a population is best served through what Neuman referred to as purposive sampling. Purposive sampling means "to select cases with a specific purpose in mind" (p. 198). Neuman indicated several reasons that a researcher would make this choice. I employed purposive sampling because my goal was to conduct an in-depth study of collaborative leaders who represent a special population: those that have been identified by others as collaborative in their approach.

Sample Size

In qualitative research, sample size is largely dependent upon one's research methodology and the end goals for the study. In most qualitative research, the goal is saturation rather than generalization. That is, the researcher is searching for depth of information (Creswell, 2013). For this reason, sample sizes are typically small. My goal for this study was to interview up to 36 individuals from two organizations, with an equal number from each. The objective was to have a population sample from each organization such that each would represent a complete study unto itself. The purpose of this strategy was to increase the credibility and dependability of the data. As discussed earlier, the purpose of exploring two organizations was to increase the credibility of the data.

The two organizations in this study are heretofore referred to as Organization A and Organization B. Twelve individuals volunteered from Organization A, thereby limiting the number of participants needed from Organization B also to 12. However, the names for 13 people were offered and therefore accepted. As discussed below, the recruitment process varied slightly between the two organizations.

Recruitment Process

My population of interest was leaders who are viewed by others to be collaborative in their practice. I contacted people within my network with whom I had previously discussed collaborative leadership and who are well networked with leaders who practice such an approach. While no precise definition was offered to these contacts, I did discuss what collaborative leadership might look like. The purpose of requiring external acknowledgement of their practice was to ensure a broader recognition and confirmation than self-nomination alone can offer. I chose to recruit leaders from within organizations that are also committed to the practice of collaborative leadership. By choosing individuals and their organizations, this allowed me to gather additional data beyond interviews, and therefore to inquire beyond the thoughts of leaders. The goal was also to explore evidence of how these leaders *act* on their thoughts of power. This was achieved by considering interactions between these leaders and their followers, as well as organizational systems and structures.

Both organizations in this study were identified through a process of peer nomination. That is, two separate individuals known to me through my professional network recommended them. They understood my search criteria, had a broad professional network at both a local and a global level, and extensive knowledge about the organizations they recommended. Of the two individuals I contacted, one was a Director General of a global professional networking organization headquartered in Europe, and the second person was a member of that same organization located in North America. His work focused on sustainability in business. In both instances, I requested recommendations of organizations that would fit my criteria. My goal was to find two organizations that were recognized for practicing collaborative leadership, for being viewed in the marketplace as successful in their sector, and for being outstanding in at least one other way. Both individuals provided me with a list of companies to consider.

I researched each of the organizations on the list and prioritized them against my criteria. I then approached my top two choices. In one case, I already had a personal contact resulting from a volunteer project that we had both worked on. In the second case, my contact introduced me to the CEO via email, and I proceeded with the recruitment process from there. Both of the organizations that agreed to participate in this study met all of my selection criteria. In terms of their being outstanding in one other way, they have been recognized in peer forums as being outstanding innovative social enterprises.

All members of Organization A were invited to participate. The goal was to find a minimum of 12 people who would agree to be interviewed. The CEO and his Executive Assistant identified the participants from Organization B. The reason for the distinction in recruiting methods is twofold. Organization A is a small organization. At the time of the study, it numbered 30 in total. Thus, it was logistically easy to correspond with the entire organization. Also, my contact person expressed a preference for people making a choice as to whether or not they wanted to participate. Organization B is a much larger organization. To get a clear picture of how the leadership functions, it was important to speak with the entire leadership team reporting to the CEO. Additionally, a few individuals at levels below this team were also considered by the CEO to be important contributors to the overall leadership of the organization. For this reason, 13 people were asked to participate. Everyone in both organizations was reminded twice that participation was voluntary and that they could withdraw at any time. No one did and all participated enthusiastically.

Data Collection

Typical of qualitative research, this study employed multiple methods for data collection (Creswell, 2013). These are semistructured interviews, organization documents, and observations of group interaction. The interviews serve as the primary data set for this study, as this is principally a study of individual leaders. The data from organizational documents and from group observations are secondary sources that serve to both complement and contrast with the interview data.

Semistructured interviews. Twenty-five people across two organizations participated in one-hour interviews via Skype (see Appendix A for a copy of the introductory letter to potential participants). The interviews were recorded and subsequently transcribed by a professional transcriptionist who was working under a signed confidentiality agreement. The interview design was informed by Greeno, Collins, and Resnick's (1996) typology of learning. These authors explored multiple learning theories, all of which could be applied to shed light on how individuals and groups construct a phenomenon such as power. Of interest here are cognitive processes, as these align with the individual or entitative aspects of this study. From a cognitive perspective, individuals learn through their interactions with the environment. These environmental interactions may or may not include direct interaction with others.

The interview was purposefully structured. I began with introductory comments to create a safe space for dialogue; I proceeded with a request for basic biographical information. The intention behind having the participants talk about themselves first was to have them develop some initial comfort with the interview process. Next, I explored each participant's narratives about power. I achieved this by asking questions that evoked stories of critical incidents in the participant's life in general and in their organizational life specifically. I then asked a series of semistructured questions. These questions comport with Moustakas' (1994) recommendation to launch the interview with questions that explore the participant's experience with the phenomenon under review (see Appendix B for the Interview Protocol).

Group observations. Greeno, Collins, and Resnick's (1996) typology of learning inspired how I approached this data source. Of interest here are collective learning theories. From a social constructionist perspective, the act of construction is understood to be the product of relationships. From this frame, the construction of knowledge is intersubjective (Dachler & Hosking, 1995). Learning occurs through engagement and is informed by the situational and historical context within which such engagement occurs. Group observation thus presents itself as a reliable approach to gathering data. It exemplifies and provides access to the intersubjective meaning-making process.

My intention was to observe a meeting where as many members as possible of each of the two proposed organizations were present. In the case of Organization A, whose members are globally distributed, I was provided with access to a video-recording of a typical Monday morning teleconferenced meeting where all available organizational members attended virtually. This meeting is regularly recorded. I surmised that Organization A was uncomfortable allowing me to observe them. After several requests, they eventually provided me with the link to the regularly recorded one-hour video staff teleconference. However, this was an information- sharing meeting. Decision-making was not part of the agenda. I was able to make useful observations about how the participants interrelate with one another, but not to the extent I had hoped for.

Organization B permitted me to be present for a regularly scheduled 2½-hour senior management team meeting. While much of this meeting was also information sharing, a discussion about an important issue did take place and their decision-making process was discernable. During the meeting, I observed from the edges of the group and did not engage in any interaction other than to introduce myself. I had already interviewed the people present at the meeting, so discussion was minimal. Following my introduction, I retreated to the background to listen and take notes of the ensuing conversation. Again, observation over a longer period of time would have been preferable but was not logistically feasible.

Systems and structures. To explore systems and structures, I reviewed corporate documentation from both organizations. In addition to reviewing documents, I captured comments about systems and structures for both organizations during the course of the interviews. Organization A provided me with eight documents that cover a range of topics from organization strategy through to a matrix of decision-making authority (see Appendix C for a listing). My contact explained that the organization only develops corporate documents on an as-needed basis. He provided all that he felt would be relevant to this research. Once I had reviewed all of the Organization A documents, I scheduled a Skype call with my contact to ask clarifying questions. My contact also used this call to share clarifying information.

While Organization B had many more formal organizational documents as compared to Organization A, fewer in number were of direct relevance to this study. During a one-day visit to the corporate head office, Organization B allowed me access to their corporate intranet. I reviewed their public website, read through their custom-designed leadership development program materials, and attended a luncheon presentation by several of the senior management team given to emerging leaders (see Appendix C for a listing of documents). At the end of my visit, I was able to spend 45 minutes with the Chief Human Resources Officer who answered questions that I had accumulated throughout my visit.

Data Analysis

Semistructured interviews. For phenomenological studies, researchers code specific statements made by participants about their lived experiences of a given phenomenon and then group these statements into clusters or themes that represent the phenomenon under review. In this study, the interview data revealed participants' thoughts and underpinning beliefs about power and, to some extent, why they hold these thoughts. I used NVivo software for data analysis and followed the procedures outlined by Richards (2009).

Broadly, the steps for handling data were to transcribe interview recordings, read through the transcriptions while listening to the recordings to check for accuracy, and then read through each interview again to summarize the major points within a memo. Following this second review of the transcripts, I wrote in my research journal about what was emerging for me from the data at this stage. Journaling is an important process in qualitative research. It serves as a vehicle for researchers to reflect on their role in generating the data for the study, and what are "the biases and interests and areas of ignorance" (Richards, 2009, p. 49).

Transcripts were then loaded in the NVivo software, where I applied five previously designated topics codes of collaborative leadership, conflict, descriptions of power, decision-making, and systems and structures. These codes were identified as important issues as a result of both a review of the literature and my previous study conducted in 2012. These codes also informed the design of the interview protocol. Decision-making was particularly chosen, as my earlier study (Davis, 2013) suggested that this action tends to be the place where the most challenges and opportunities exist for the exercise of power.

Once all of the interviews were coded by topic, I performed in-depth analytical coding. I looked for common themes that could be combined and overly dense themes that needed to be broken down further into new codes. While engaging in this process, my focus shifted between coding and reflecting on what was emerging for me from this coding. All procedures and reflections were captured in memos and were logged in my research journal.

When the coding was complete, I read through the themes and summarized my thoughts about each of them in my journal. These last steps provided the juncture where theory began to emerge and key findings were first identified. Lastly, I reviewed the journal and began the process of theory development in relation to the coded interview data. This is an iterative process, requiring several reviews of the journal, sometimes returning to the original coding and simultaneous journaling to reach a point where the analysis felt complete.

Group observation. I selected an ethnographic lens for the analysis of these data. The data include a video-recorded teleconference, approximately one hour in length, of an all-staff meeting for Organization A. Also included is a 2½-hour senior management meeting for Organization B; this I observed in person.

While reviewing the video recording, I captured specific quotes and made extensive notes, including minute details about aspects such as tone of voice, facial expressions, and speech pauses. I reviewed the recording approximately four times, adding to my notes on each review. Once my review of the video was complete, I wrote extensive field notes to record aspects such as the interactions among participants such as who appeared to be central to the dialogue and who appeared to be peripheral.

Following the meeting with Organization B, I had approximately 30 minutes alone. I found a quiet place and made notes about what I had observed in the meeting. In terms of data analysis, I followed a similar process to that with Organization A, but with much more limited data. The next step entailed writing reflexive memos to interpret the meaning of the meeting interactions. I also noted my personal reactions to what I had observed. Journaling represents a critical activity throughout the data collection and analysis processes in order to both make sense of the data and foreground my assumptions and biases.

The next stage entailed identifying patterns and themes that emerged from the data. Sangasubana (2011) recommends coding for descriptive labels and then sorting for patterns. I prioritized themes that provided insights into power dynamics. Throughout this process, I also looked for comments or interactions that did not fit with the rest of my observations.

Systems and structures. Ethnography guided the analysis of the documented systems and structures, and Giddens's (1984, 1991) structuration theory provided the inspiration for including these data as part of the study.[8] Giddens's intention was to build a bridge over the divide that separates paradigms. His theory serves to link the subject/object split by offering a perspective on how social actors are at once the creators of their social systems and, at the same time, created by them. Giddens proposes that action creates systems and structures and is also a product of them. He views these systems and structures as the outcomes of established practices that inform the influences found in social life (Giddens, 1993). This dynamic interaction represents what Giddens refers to as the duality of agency and structure. Neither agency nor structure is privileged in shaping human action; they are seen as complementary forces.

The primary interest in including systems and structures as part of this study was to understand how they serve to reinforce or contradict the findings that emerged from an analysis of the semistructured interviews. As a stand-alone body of evidence, these texts represent the intention of its authors. My central question in reviewing them was whether or not the leaders have created systems and structures to support and reinforce how they think about power. A secondary question was whether these documents provide new or contradictory insights.

Following completion of the interview data analysis, I read through the organizational documents several times. Each reading, I highlighted and recorded themes and patterns. Once I felt I had saturated the analysis, I sorted for themes relevant to the research question. While I was influenced by the themes identified in the interview data, I remained vigilant for any new insights and contradictions. I captured the insights on an Excel spreadsheet and then summarized the findings in my research journal.

Synthesis

Once I had completed the data analysis for all three sources, I then compared and contrasted the findings. I was able to find common themes and reinforcements for the primary findings resulting from the interview data. I also discovered some new and useful findings in both the documents and the group observations that both provide further insights into how these leaders construct power and indicate areas of contradiction. These findings are presented in Chapter 4 and discussed in detail in Chapter 5.

Pilot Study

The purpose of the pilot study was to test the efficacy of the study design. That is, did it produce the sort and quality of data that the study was designed to generate? While three data sets were collected for the main study, the pilot study tested only the interview protocol and resultant data. This decision was made for several reasons. First, because this is primarily an entitative study, the interview data are considered the primary source of data. Second, it was beyond the scope of the pilot study to test the other two data sets. To do so would have required engaging an entire organization in order to consider both group observations and systems and structural information. This was neither feasible nor logistically possible.

There were two participants in the pilot study, both of whom met the individual selection criteria for the main study. Both worked in organizations that practice a collaborative approach to leadership and had served as participants in my earlier study of collaborative leaders (Davis, 2013). In that study, I knew one through my professional networks, and one was recruited through a snowball process where participants recommended additional participants.

The findings of the pilot study comport well with the power literature. Comments about the three locutions of power, as discussed in Chapter 2, were easily identifiable, and participant views of each of these expressions of power aligned with my expectations. For example, both participants were opposed to the use of power-over or power as dominance. Even when it seems necessary, such as when there is time pressure, they preferred not to use power-over. However, they both recognized that the use of power as dominance is sometimes needed. Asked to tell a story about when they used power in a way that had ill effects, their narratives were about non-collaborative decision-making. Neither of the participants felt positive about this use of power.

The participants' view of the importance of using power-with paralleled how it is conceived of in Karlberg's schema reviewed in Chapter 2. When there is inequality in the relationship, the leader's role is to draw forth the follower's potential through some form of enablement, empowerment, and/or accompaniment. Rather than framing empowerment as an act of endowing power, the participants viewed empowerment as a drawing forth of the capacity for power that already exists with the follower. The ultimate goal was to create an environment where everyone is working to his or her highest potential and greatest capacities.

The findings of the pilot study indicated that the interview design was robust in that it elicited the types and quality of data that are sought. Some minor modifications to the interview protocol were identified and reviewed with my Committee Chair. They were subsequently added to the design.

Protection of Human Participants

Institutional Review Board norms were followed. All participants were informed of the purpose of the study, the approach being used, and my commitment to personal and organizational confidentiality. This includes the use of pseudonyms for both the participants and the organizations. Participants were advised that all personal information collected would be protected, and shared only with members of the Fielding Graduate University community that serve on my committee. Participants provided an electronic signature for their informed consent forms (see Appendix D for a sample Informed Consent Form). No one in this study represented a vulnerable population. No identifying information will be published. All participants took part in the study voluntarily and were advised of their right to withdraw at any time without consequence. Interviews were captured via audio recordings and were transcribed by a transcription service that signed a confidentiality agreement. All data are kept within password-protected computer files.

Trustworthiness of Study Findings

Noble and Smith (2015) observed that qualitative research is frequently criticized for the lack of transparency in the methods employed, researcher bias in identifying and interpreting findings, and the lack of scientific rigour. The standards tests of validity and reliability employed in quantitative research do not apply. Lincoln and Guba's (1985) advice to establish credibility, transferability, dependability, and confirmability are still the gold standards that researchers seek to measure their work against. Credibility means the reader can have confidence in the truth of the findings. Transferability means the findings can be applied in other contexts, and dependability means the findings are both consistent throughout and repeatable. Confirmability means that the findings are reflective of the participants' bias and not the researcher's bias, motivations, or personal interests.

Noble and Smith (2015) recommended a number of

strategies to aid researchers in achieving these standards. Of the nine strategies listed, I worked to achieve eight. As discussed below, one was unattainable in this study. Following is a review of how those strategies were applied in this study. The first and second strategies are to account for bias. In terms of personal bias, I acknowledged mine in Chapter 1 in the section devoted to assumptions. I also engaged in critical reflection through regular journaling. I acknowledge any biases in sampling in the section devoted to study limitations.

The third strategy is to maintain meticulous records. I regularly wrote in my research journal to capture my experience of working with the research data and allow for reflection on methods. I adhered to methods of data analysis as prescribed by Richards (2009) to ensure accuracy and repeatability by other researchers. I also documented each step in my processes.

The fourth strategy includes seeking both similarities and differences in the data. I did find distinctions and highlight those in Chapter 4. The fifth strategy is to include "rich and thick verbatim descriptions of participants' accounts" (Noble & Smith, 2015, p. 35). These are extensively used in Chapter 4. The sixth strategy is to demonstrate clarity of thought during analysis and interpretation of data. This will be for the reader to judge. However, the time and effort to ensure care in these two areas represents the largest investment of my time.

The seventh strategy requires one to engage with other researchers to reduce bias. I held regular calls with my Committee Chair and with two colleagues where discussions about process and interpretation of findings were the primary topics. I also engaged an external examiner to review the entire study. The eighth strategy is to invite study participants to validate the data. I chose to not follow this step for logistical reasons. The ninth and final strategy is to employ data triangulation. While the purpose of collecting documentation and observing participants engaging with one another served to fulfill a design goal, it also helped to validate the primary data gathered through interviews, and to produce a comprehensive set of findings.

Summary

This chapter outlined the research design for this study. The epistemological framework, theoretical perspectives, methodologies, and methods that informed the data collection and analysis were explained in detail. A central contention of this study is that construction is both an entitative and a relational act. That is, it requires both thought and action to be fully constituted. Data were collected from three sources. Evidence of the participants' thoughts about power was obtained through semistructured interviews. Group observations provided insights into how these leaders construct power while in action, as dialogue is a form of action. Systems and structures represent both thoughts and intentions to act. To explore systems and structures, data were collected and analyzed from corporate documents (see Appendix C). The data from all three sources were coded into themes to allow for theory building and cross- comparisons. Finally, the actions taken to protect the human participants and to ensure the trustworthiness of data were reviewed. Chapter 4 presents the key findings of the study identified through the methods reviewed in this chapter.

CHAPTER FOUR

KEY FINDINGS

The purpose of this study is to expand our understanding of collaborative leadership. It achieves this by exploring how leaders who are identified as collaborative construct power. Power was chosen as the focus for the inquiry because it is fundamental to leadership (Tjosvold & Wisse, 2009). These two phenomena have been conflated in the literature to the extent that they are frequently thought to be synonymous with one another. Power is also a concept that is not well studied in the context of collaborative approaches to leadership (Bolden, 2011; Denis et al., 2012; Gronn, 2008).

This chapter presents the key findings. They were developed through observations of group interactions of both organizations, and an analysis of the various data including interview transcripts, documents, and comments from interviews about organizational systems and structures. The primary data of interest are the interview transcripts. The secondary data provide additional evidence to support the interviews, as well as new insights. When combined with the interview data, they also aid in generating a more holistic perspective on how these collaborative leaders construct power.

This chapter begins with an introduction to the two organizations and to the study participants, followed by an overview of the key findings from the interview data. These findings have been sorted into themes and subthemes, supported by direct quotes from the participants. Next, the key findings from an analysis of group observations and systems and structures are presented. These are also sorted into themes. The final section of this chapter presents surprising and contrary findings that were identified in each of the data sources.

Study Participants

Twenty-five people from two organizations were interviewed for this study. An overview of both organizational and participant information is provided below and summarized in Table 1. Only summary data have been provided, in order to protect the anonymity of both the study participants and the two organizations they represent. These organizations are referred to as Organization A and Organization B. Organization A is a global consulting firm. At the time of the interviews, the staff comprised partners, associates, and full-time and part-time contractors situated on four continents and serving clients located around the globe. Twelve participants from Organization A volunteered to be interviewed. These 12 represented the partner or senior management team (5), the associate level (5), and contractors (2). My contact person for this organization was a partner.

This partner requested that I invite two contractors to be interviewed because of their high level of participation in the organization. One contractor was functioning as a full-time Associate and has since been established as such. His responses were rich as similar to his full-time peers. The second contractor is also a senior leader in a large networked organization and has extensive background in both the theory and practice of leadership. He provided valuable insights about the use of power that tended to parallel the partner perspectives.

The majority of the people from Organization A were leaders of people. That is, some part of their role required that they lead others. Six of the participants were leaders as a formal part of their job, while others served as project managers assuming a leadership role from time to time. The two exceptions were a contractor who had recently begun working with the organization, and a contractor who serves as a leader in his home organization. That organization also practices collaborative leadership. The people led by the participants represented varying constituencies. For example, they may have been employees or contractors of Organization A, employees of client organizations, or individuals that were associated with, but at arm's length from, client organizations. This final category may have comprised people from the public who had volunteered to participate in projects that Organization A was responsible to coordinate.

Table 1

Summary of Study Participants' Background Information

Characteristics	n
Gender	
Female	12
Male	13
Age	
25 – 29	1
30 – 34	3
35 – 39	4

40 – 44	3
45 – 49	8
50 – 54	2
55 – 59	3
60 – 65	1
Terminal Degree	
No degree	1
BA/BS	13
BBA/BCom/CA	3
MBA/MA	3
JD	1
MD	1
PhD	3
Early Childhood Living Experiences	
North America (Canada, USA, Mexico)	15
South America	3
Asia	2
South Africa	2
United Kingdom	2
Europe	1
Extent of Cross-cultural Experiences	
Extensive	21
Limited	4

Note. An extensive cross-cultural experience indicates either living and/or working in another culture for an extended period of time, or having multiple years of experience engaging and socializing directly with other cultures (e.g., First Nations communities, immigrant populations). Many of the participants have lived on more than one continent. Continents represented include North America, South America, Africa, and Asia.

Of the 12 people from Organization A that volunteered to participate in this study, 5 are female and 7 are male. They range in age from 24 to 50 with the majority being from 35 to 44 years of age. All participants hold at least one degree and nine have postgraduate degrees, including one MA, three MBAs, one JD, one MD, and three PhDs. All of the participants from Organization A have experienced many cultures, mostly as a result of living on more than one continent at some point in their lives. Generally, this occurred in early childhood. Where this is not the case, the participants may have engaged extensively with other cultures as part of their social life.

Organization B is a nation-wide retail organization designed around a member-owned cooperative governance structure. It boasts a worldwide membership of over four million people. The employees who were interviewed were situated in three locations including the head office, a regional office, and a store. All but one of them had a role that focused on the entire enterprise. All participants were people leaders within the organization, representing four levels of management. Participants included the CEO (1), his direct reports on the senior leadership team (7), direct reports to the senior leadership team (4), and a store manager (1). Of the 13 participants, 7 are female and 6 are male. They range in age from 34 to 65 with the majority being 40 to 49 years of age. All but one holds an undergraduate degree. In terms of multicultural experiences, similar to Organization A, almost all of the participants have lived and/or worked on more than one continent.

Demographic information has been provided detached from other identifying information to ensure that participant anonymity is maintained. All the participants have been assigned with a pseudonym to further protect their identity. Appendix E identifies the participants in terms of their pseudonyms, organizational affiliations, and organizational levels.

In terms of my relationship to the study participants,

the majority were unknown to me prior to this study. I had interviewed four of the participants in a previous study of collaborative leaders (Davis, 2013), only two of which were working with one of this study's participant organizations at that time. Of the other two, one was employed elsewhere and one became a contractor. I had professional dealings with two of these four people, both of whom had assisted me in finding participants for this study. Prior to visiting Organization A, I have physically met only one of the participants with whom I have had contact on a professional basis.

Key Findings

This study represents the first empirical inquiry into how collaborative leaders construct power. It is a qualitative study employing thematic analysis of the research data. The key findings are organized under six themes, and supported by 19 subthemes, as outlined in Table 2. The first three themes of reflecting on power, using power, and abusing power focus on how the leaders in this study think about power. These three themes represent the nucleus of understanding about how leaders in this study construct power.

Identifying and exploring power is no simple task. Power is not something that is tangible. It must be inferred from evidence. As a result, supporting evidence assumes a special place of importance when substantiating findings about power. To this end, this study considers three additional themes as confirmation of leaders' thoughts about power. They also serve the additional purpose of broadening our understanding of the beliefs and guiding principles that inform these leaders' constructions of power.

Table 2

Themes and Subthemes

Research question	Nature of the construction	Theme	Subtheme
How do leaders who are identified as collaborative construct power?	Thinking about power	Reflecting on power	1. Power is a neutral force 2. Constructions of power are learned
		Using power	1. Inspiring 2. Releasing capacity 3. Role modeling
		Abusing power	1. Using power against 2. Gender differences
	Acting on power	Relational equality	1. Shared leadership 2. Participatory decision-making 3. Respect for others 4. Practice transparency
		Innovating strategic frameworks	1. Principle-centered 2. Values-based 3. Founded on collaboration 4. Devolved leadership 5. Prioritizes doing social good

Sustaining constructions of power	Shaping the environment	1. Leadership practices 2. Character 3. Culture

The fourth theme reveals how relational equality is promoted within the two organizations. This finding was evident through analyses of group interactions. The fifth theme explores innovative strategic frameworks common to both of the organizations in the study. Data for this theme were gathered through an analysis of organizational documents and unprompted comments about organizational systems and structures that participants offered during the interviews. The sixth, and final, theme provides insights into how the participants supported their constructions of power by shaping and sustaining organizational environments. The emphasis shifts away from strictly exploring thoughts to also considering actions. Subthemes examine leadership practices, leader character, and the nature of the culture they endeavor to shape. Exploring both leader thoughts and actions is essential to fully understanding how power is being constructed.

The above six themes were identified through thematic analysis of data gathered from three sources including interviews, organizational documents, and group observations. Interview data consisted of over 25 hours of interview transcripts that produced 72 distinct codes. The evidence reported here was derived almost entirely from categories that represented at least 50% of the participant population, and in more than one case represented 100 % of the participant population. This threshold was chosen due to the extent and richness of the data collected. Where findings are not present in comments made by 50 % or more of the population, they have been identified as such. Efforts were made to present evenly distributed participant comments from across the two organizations to illuminate the findings. Where this is not the case, and responses are more reflective of one organization over the other, this fact has been highlighted.

A second approach was to observe and analyze group interactions in each of the organizations. Organization A provided me with a recorded video teleconference of a staff meeting, and Organization B allowed me to physically observe their regular Monday morning senior management meeting. A third approach to analysis consisted of a review of documented organizational systems and procedures. The themes derived from this approach were compared to the themes from the interview analysis. Finally, all of the data were reviewed for contradictions. The primary one identified was follower perceptions of leader power, where followers appear to project power onto the leaders. This finding is discussed following a review of the six primary themes.

There are numerous themes that were not reported. Either the sample size did not meet the threshold for inclusion, or the themes did not sufficiently address the research question. For example, participants were asked to define collaborative leadership. The purpose of this question was to ensure that everyone was reporting on the same or a similar phenomenon. While the responses indicated a common understanding about what collaborative leadership means, the analysis did not sufficiently relate to the research question to warrant being reported.

Theme 1: Reflecting on Power

The first theme is comprised of findings that reveal how participants reflected on power as an instrument of leadership. Apart from how they defined power, many participants also expressed the ways in which they thought about and responded to power. There are two subthemes: a) power is a neutral force, and b) constructions of power are learned. These subthemes and their associated findings are summarized in Table 3, followed by a discussion and relevant quotes from participants.

Power is a neutral force. The first finding indicates that participants believed power could be expressed in both positive and negative terms. Sixteen of 25 participants made comments indicating the essential neutrality of power and the flexibility with which it can be expressed. They viewed power to be a neutral force that manifests according to one's intentions.

Table 3

Theme 1: Reflecting on Power

Subtheme	Key findings
1. Power is a neutral force	Power can be expressed in both positive and negative terms
	Expressions of power are a matter of choice
2. Constructions of power are learned	Defining experiences change perspectives on power

Benjamin suggested that we "not look at [power] as necessarily a negative thing . . . it's more neutral and it can be used positively or used negatively." Similarly, Robert said, "I think there's an easy way to spin it where it can be considered something negative as well, but I think power is a neutral work." Rosemary commented on how she views power in both positive and negative terms:

> I don't know why I have the two different definitions of power but, to me the most powerful people are people that are inspiring, encouraging, and that

there's a seamless transition between their level in the organization and the people that are underneath that organization. It's not power over people, to me that's a dictatorship, that's a negative thing.

Malcolm indicated that he holds a similar perspective when he said,

> I could speak to individuals that use it in what I would determine to be the right way in regards to influencing people, and then I've seen people use it the wrong way in which it becomes something that is threatening . . . you can manage by fear, by using power as a threat, and that could be a threat of your job.

The second finding indicates that how one expresses power is a matter of choice. While 13 of 25 participants specifically talked about choice, many of the other participants implied its importance. Malcolm stated,

> I think it is whatever you choose it to be . . . It's how you choose to use it. And so, you know, it's just that whole dynamic that really collaboration, power, it all comes down to the individual and we all get to choose in how we use that level of power.

On a similar note, Dexter commented on the importance of intentions behind one's actions, where intention is understood to be an expression of choice. He said, "I think the intentions that lie behind, whether you want to have things improve, help the person to improve, help the person to step up, that intention is very important." The participants were thoughtful about how they choose to use power, and many were also reflective about how they arrived at their choice, as is evidenced in the next findings.

Constructions of power are learned. In the second

subtheme of reflecting on power, 18 of 25 participants recalled a defining moment, experience, or event that caused them to redefine how they think about power. In all cases, the shift they experienced was moving away from using power as domination and toward using power for mutual benefit.

Samantha shaped her conceptions of power at a young age. While researching for a school project, she learned about events during the partition of India. In particular, she learned how the British Viceroy sent only Mahatma Gandhi to Calcutta to calm the citizens of that entire city, but sent whole armies to quell the riots in others. Samantha recalled, "I talked about that as power. And, I think, going through the process of thinking about that and writing about that as a young person, very much influenced how I've thought about power since then." Kolten learned from reflecting on his own actions.

> In one case I was influenced by, you know, when I would try to get people to do a particular thing I always tended to feel that it would deteriorate relationships.
>
> And it almost felt like you were expending something that was limited. And so you either had to be simultaneously gaining more authority and gaining more something that you were then expending by getting people to follow that something.

Carl relayed a similar story about using the power of his position to bully others.

> It comes back to the golden rule, where I realized that I'd be really pissed off if somebody spoke to me that way, regardless of where the power balance was in a situation. So that, for me, was pretty—that was, kind of, a watershed moment, and I've tried to deal with everybody as a collaborator and a peer, across the table, rather than sizing up okay, what's the power

balance in this conversation. And so, I can behave like a different character as a result.

Hannah changed her views about power as a result of observing others. She told the story of the president of a former organization whom she admired and learned from.

> I think I was more like bull in a china shop kind of using position to achieve a result. And realized you can't sustain that or you don't get the best result. There's better ways. So through observing people who were very successful in their roles, like people like [female president] right? . . . I watched her and I watched the power she had but she didn't say "I'm the president you have to do it my way." I watched how she achieved things . . . that's how I learned over the years you know and I'm still learning.

While the process of gaining new insights about power varied across the participant group, the net result was the same. Through reflection, they recognized that power can be manifested in more than one way; it can be used as an instrument of domination, or it can be used for purposes of mutual gain. This realization motivated them to use power as a positive force.

Theme 2: Using Power

When asked how they would define power, or when asked to recall a story of power used to positive effect, the primary term that participants used to describe power was *influencing*. They described influencing at a more granular level through three closely related motivations: a) inspiring, b) releasing capacity, and c) role modeling. These are summarized in Table 4.

Table 4

Theme 2: Using Power

Subthemes	Key findings
1. Inspiring	Inspiring means to move others toward an idea by guiding and motivating
	The direction of influence is toward the greater good
2. Releasing capacity	Providing resources, encouraging, and supporting
	Generating a sense of ownership and group unity
3. Role modeling	Role modeling means walking the talk
	Leaders learn by observing others

Inspiring. Twenty-two of 25 participants made comments that relate to this subtheme. The first finding indicates that they used power in the sense of drawing or guiding others toward an idea, as opposed to pushing or using any kind of force. In this regard, Henry said,

> I think power means the ability to influence people's thoughts and behavior in a voluntary way, meaning not in a coerced way but some of your ability to inspire them, to motivate them, to—for them to want to do the things that you would also like to see happen. I think that's power.

In a similar fashion, Malcolm stated, "What I choose to do is to influence by going in, reinforcing the things that they're doing well, but then highlighting the opportunities for improvement. And to me, that's a big differentiator in terms of the use of power." To demonstrate his meaning, he continued with a story of a mentoring conversation he had with a leader who was intimidating staff by focusing exclusively on her criticisms.

She just assumed that they knew what was right, you know, but then for me to influence her it became a very easy conversation of saying, you know, if you reinforce and praise what they're doing well, it only takes a second. Like to walk by something and go, you guys, this looks fantastic, thank you so much, way to go, you nailed this one, then you move on to the opportunity. It's a whole different way to influence people and provide leadership than only pointing out what is wrong.

Benjamin talked about one of the Partners' ability to inspire others within the organizations. He said,

He's following his kind of mode of being and beliefs in the world. It brings him to a place of really listening to people and then showing them a way of looking at things . . . and inspires them to action or inspires them to change behavior or inspires them to move forward in some kind of way.

Carl explained why inspiring others is so important.

No, I've never heard, in 20 years, anyone at Organization B say "get it done just because I said, or do it this way because I said, I'm in charge." I don't think anyone's ever said anything in that vein in an Organization B office, so what it means is, as a leader at Organization B, you need to be able to rely on influence. You need to be able to move people along, convince them, tap into their passions, draw them into a collaborative model, without just saying you have to because you have to. So, it's tricky.

Kolten spoke in terms of influencing the environment. He said, "I think that my thinking has definitely gone from . . . authority or the ability to kind of choose your outcome to more of understanding power as your ability to influence the environment within which outcomes happen." To illustrate his point he offered the example of how one of his peer leaders influences behavior within the organization: "He engages in a particular type of behavior. And, because he does, he enlists the rest of us in engaging in that type of behavior. You can see it influencing the entire organization."

The direction these leaders inspire others is toward the greater good, and is in no way self-serving. Nerita reflected, "I think here you can say that this power is more looking to influence for the greater whole than to influence for one individual's well-being." The words and phrases these leaders used to describe what inspiring means included creating an environment, enabling people to feel powerful in their positions, encouraging, engaging the group in an inclusive way, facilitating, guiding, motivating, supporting, and promoting collaboration. These uplifting terms suggest an objective of drawing out follower capacity or potential. In this way, the subtheme of influencing is closely related to releasing capacity.

Releasing capacity. Twenty-two of 25 participants contributed comments to this subtheme. Their remarks offered a perspective on why they showed a preference for *drawing people toward* as opposed to the typical definition of *exerting influence on*. It is also notable that these leaders tended to avoid what might be construed as invasive interventions. Instead, they employed a lighter approach by choosing to provide resources, encouraging others to find the motivation to act within themselves, and then supporting their followers in taking action.

Benjamin explained,

> When you're managing people it's more about working with folks as individuals and helping them grow for their own sake . . . If I'm a good manager that means

that I am serving them by supporting them and being better and growing and strengthening their skills and achieving what they want to achieve. I see that if I can do that successfully then I am essentially extending the impact that I can have on the world by building up the ability for others to have that impact.

Hannah uses similar language to describe her approach.

I don't think that's healthy to be directive as the leader. I'm one of the, "I'm a servant leader, I work for them." So my whole thing is to get the big rocks out of their way and let them come up with the ideas. I'd like them to become more entrepreneurial and making more decisions with less fear.

Rachel said, "I think the other thing about power is it's also the ability to . . . stay in the background and let other people get out in front and support them."

A primary reason that they chose to use this approach was to generate a sense of ownership and feeling of group unity. Dexter explained that the senior leaders in his organization have "a sincere wish to help everybody else excel and be successful . . . making sure that everybody looks great, performs great . . . and we all feel very much part in owning this way forward." Robert observed that followers will have "a lot more strength because they know that they were part of the choice and therefore that they also have some of the responsibility to make it work." Selma stated,

I think that you want people to unify and once again to feel that there is some democracy that people have a voice. That people are not just demanded to do something. I think when you do collaborate I think there is trust in the process that says that your opinion counts.

Dorothy cautioned that moving too quickly can have negative implications such as people becoming dependent upon the leader for confirmations "rather than thinking about what's the best solution and putting forward the solutions." When this occurred, she tried to steer people and then back away again as soon as possible by "[giving] them a framework rather than all the details."

As with most things, there is a shadow side to releasing capacity. Ross shared a story about a person who rallied people around her to gossip about another, subsequently creating a toxic environment for everyone. Her negative behavior modeled the way for others to behave in a like manner. How a leader manifests power is typically observed by others, thus the leader needs to be conscious that they are always being observed and role modeling behavior.

Role modeling. The subtheme of role modeling is also closely related to inspiring and releasing capacity. Thirteen of 25 participants made comments about role modeling, speaking of it in purposeful terms such as *walking the talk*. Rosemary said, "to me, power in an organization is somebody that can lead by example." Garth stated, "I think that power sort of expresses itself in a leader maybe demonstrating a behavior and then everybody else picking up on that behavior." Kolten built on his earlier story of influencing and related it to role modeling when he explained that his colleague

> engages in a type of behavior and enlists the rests of us in engaging in that type of behavior. You can see it influencing the entire organization . . . modeling a behavior as opposed to mandating something or forcing somebody else to do it.

Farren spoke of her own purposeful role modeling when she stopped engaging with others during the weekend with the goal of "[giving] people permission to not always be on."

Other participants talked about how they learned by observing how others modeled leadership and the use of power. Henry described how he learned from an important role model in his life and how he put this learning into effect in his own life.

She exercised power by walking the talk. It was like Gandhi said, be the change you seek to create. So, she embodied a change in her and that had a tremendous pulling power because I got inspired by what she does and not only me but the group got inspired and wanted to follow. So that kind of embodiment and inspiration of power, it's very effective.

When Henry wanted to effect change in his organization he adopted this same approach. His goal was to "create a different kind of power, the power of prototyping the changes that I want to create. So that it becomes a reality and people see the possibility and maybe more willing to shift to that new state."

Hannah talked about two important role models in her career.

I watched her and I watched the power she had but she didn't say I'm the president you have to do it my way. I watched how she achieved things . . . that's how I learned over the years . . . and I'm still learning. I watch [our CEO] and I watch how he integrates with groups and I'm like "wow this is a whole different level."

Malcolm made a similar claim when he said, "I really respect [our CEO] for how he uses his power . . . treats everybody with respect." Leaders need not be observed in the present moment. Participants also mentioned historical and iconic figures such as Mahatma Gandhi and Nelson Mandela whom they have learned from.

These leaders recognized the importance of self-awareness, particularly in terms of how their behavior might influence others. Farren commented on the shadow side of role modeling when she observed, "if leaders aren't paying attention, their behaviors and the way that they do things, because they are in a position of power, [they] negatively influence things." As an example of the importance of self-awareness, Hannah self-disclosed that she may have "trampled on a few people . . . I discouraged some people who maybe wanted to be leaders." Participants talked about these negative recollections with regret.

Theme 3: Abusing Power

When asked to share stories about the ineffective use of power, participants a) spoke of using power against another, and b) demonstrated gender differences in how they believe they personally abuse power. The first subtheme addresses shared stories that were either about dominating others in some manner, or about constraining others such that these others were prevented from accessing their full potential. While the two findings are closely related, there is an important distinction between them. Participants relayed that dominating represents a behavior, while being constrained is a felt experience by the person being dominated.

The second subtheme relates to issues of gender in the abuse of power. While there was no particular intention to explore gender issues, participant responses indicate that it is an important topic worthy of discussion. Two findings emerged that relate to gender. The first one concerned males believing they abuse power through overuse, while females believed they abused power through underuse. The subthemes and related findings are summarized in Table 5.

Table 5

Theme 3: Abusing Power

Subthemes	Key findings
1. Using power against	Dominating others Constraining others
2. Gender differences	Males abuse power through overuse
	Females abuse power through underuse

Using power against. Not unexpectedly, what participants considered being the abuse of power is the mirror opposite of how they described the effective use of power. As Ross commented, "it's actually stopping the release of capacity." Abusing power means that a leader dominates others in a manner that results in feelings on the part of followers of being constrained or limited from the full expression of their capacities. Twenty-three of 25 participants offered stories in which power was categorized as either dominating or constraining others. These stories were not necessarily about how participants themselves abused power; rather, they were largely stories about what they themselves had experienced or observed regarding the abuse of power.

Domination manifests as behavior ranging from being directive through to being coercive.

Holly shared a story about a leader being directive that her spouse had experienced.

> He had worked in a retail giant store at points and it's very discouraging and miserable for everyone who works there when the regional manager calls into the store on a Wednesday and says, "You guys are not selling enough this week. I need you to cut 40 hours

from the schedule between now and Saturday." So all of a sudden, the manager is forced to make a decision about whose hours she's going to cut in order to meet this person's requirements. Who is not going to get their kids shoes, who is not going to get their macaroni and cheese money to get them through college or whatever it is.

The behavior associated with the abuse of power can be as simple as talking negatively about others behind their backs to outright verbal abuse. Holly described this latter case when she continued with another example from the same organization:

My husband has talked about calls on which he was involved where the manager would humiliate various managers in the region on these calls on purpose just to make them feel bad for something that's going wrong in their location in front of the rest of the managers. To me, that is definitely to ill effect because it's dehumanizing, demoralizing and definitely does not generate loyalty and the kind of attitude toward work that's going to generate a thriving and prosperous business.

While the nature of the behavior that is viewed as abusive varies from story to story, what does not alter is the extent to which others feel constrained, diminished, or limited by the dominating behavior or the toxicity that is subsequently created in the environment. In the majority of the stories, the participants did not feel they had done anything to invite this abusive behavior. Participants viewed the abuser's motivation to be rooted in issues of ego. Lawrence underlined this point of view when he said, "I think power is always used to ill effect if it's attached to ego and your own personal gain." Similarly, Rosemary stated, "When I think of power, I think of ego and dictatorship."

Constraint is generally understood to be the direct result of feeling dominated by another. For example, Henry said,

> His power was very non-dialogic and was very authoritarian, was very "I know better than you and just follow my lead" and a hierarchical way of being, very dominating way of making decisions. So, working the three months I felt so out of place and so resistant to his style of leadership that I just quit without a single regret.

Henry continued on to explain, "what was going on for me was I don't feel I was seen or respected as an equal human being. In that environment I don't thrive." In his example, the leader behaved in an authoritarian manner, telling people what to do rather than engaging them in dialogue. Nerita shared a similar story of being verbally abused. As a result, she said, "I was afraid of him for the rest of the time that I worked there." Hannah talked about the behavior of a new CEO in the retail organization where she worked who

> cut all the frontline little bonus programs and recognition programs because they cost too much money. [The new CEO] gave every president of every division a brand new BMW, took great big trips. Like he was just everything about ugly corporate America.

The cost of power abuse is high. Malcolm said,

> The best people will only do that for a certain amount of time and then they'll make the decision that they don't want to live their lives or treat other people the same way and they'll move on to other things. So, you know, like I said, I think people that get results using power in a threatening manner, typically the results are short-term and short-lived.

Tyrone reflected that "people sort of lived in fear, but there was no trust and there was no sense of you know, I'm buying into this guy's vision and I will support him." Kolten observed, "leaders who have surrounded themselves with people that agree with them and it's such a tragedy and a travesty . . . you lose a tremendous opportunity for growth." Benjamin reported on the consequences of his own actions when he said, "the way that I set the course was much more directive than consultative and it frustrated my team as a result." And Holly observed, "I feel like in general it can harm the relationship."

Ultimately, such behavior is not viewed as leadership. Henry stated, "you can just coerce people through your authority, which is different from leadership." He went on to say, "I am so curious how can somebody preach one thing and act another way; it is just mind-boggling to me."

Conversely, some of the participants believed that directive behavior is occasionally warranted, so long as one's purpose is to positively motivate another. Dexter talked about an incident where he felt he needed to be directive.

> Being direct sounds like really bad, I think, at times, can actually be done—with certain individuals can actually be very, very positive. So the bad thing is losing my patience and sending very straight and very annoyed email communications to people at times, which causes the wrong kind of reactions… I'm learning the positive and the negative, that being very direct and really pushing people in the right way for the right reasons can actually be beneficial.

In a similar vein, Dorothy disclosed,

> I don't like using the "I'm the boss" card… I think there's always those times where, like I said, I will pull out, if I have to, I'll pull out the card of "no, that's not

acceptable"... it's not something that you constantly do, because it has an ill effect on staff morale.

However, when the use of domination was motivated by ego, or some other negative motivation, the effects on the perpetrator can also feel negative. Kolten shared a personal example:

> When I would try to get people to do a particular thing I always tended to feel that it would deteriorate relationships. And it almost felt like you were expending something that was limited. And so you either had to be simultaneously gaining more authority and gaining more something that you were then expending by getting people to follow that something.

Gender issues. Eleven of 25 participants made comments that shed light on gender distinctions in terms of the use of power. Of these, males made four comments and females made seven comments. While the number of comments did not meet the analysis threshold of 50% of participants, they were noteworthy. A review of the responses indicates that males feel they abuse power through overuse. For example, Kolten said,

> You want your conversations to hold based on the validity of your ideas as opposed to the authority of your position. And, I would say that when your point of view is used—when the defense of your arguments is your seniority that would be an example of power used to extreme ill effect . . . early on in my career I did that a couple of times . . . and it was actually really good to do that because it—I remember the taste of it.

When females discussed stories about their abuse of power they reported either not using it enough or not using it at all. Farren said, "I think I sometimes underestimate the power that I have because my thinking is that I'm trying to operate much more in a collaborative type of setting." She later shared a story where she believed she underused her power, when she was

> not following kind of my gut or my business instinct on things, and trying to go along with almost kind of the flow or the consensus. And so, I want to say that's kind of an unconscious thing or maybe it was the conscious decision to not follow it and it ended up in negative outcomes on things that I should have known better on. So, I almost think in my case it's more the avoidance of not digging in when I needed to.

Rosemary offered a similar story. She talked about

> not making a decision fast enough. So, maybe, dragging it out a little bit too long in order to … 1) either I wasn't sure of the decision myself, or 2) hoping and thinking that things were just going to blow over and they didn't. So, there are times when I probably just said, "Just keep going. Just keep doing what you're doing" and not stepped in soon enough to solve the problems.

Some of the females do not even acknowledge their ability to access power. Selma said, "power is not a word that I would use. I would never say I have power," and Nerita declared, "I don't think of myself as someone who has a lot of power." This is not to suggest that the male participants dwell on their having access to power. For example, Lawrence stated, "This is something I don't often think about."

A few of the female participants shared stories of using power forcefully, but when they did, it was only in the context of having positive intentions. That is, they were consciously choosing to use power forcefully because they firmly believed a positive outcome required them to do so. A few of the male participants offered stories where they were not accessing power. However, in general, the males tended to view themselves as abusing power when they overused it, and the females viewed themselves as abusing power when they failed to use it.

Theme 4: Relational Equality

Theme 4 continues the exploration of the construction of power, but through a different lens than leaders' thoughts. The data for this theme were gathered through observations of group interactions. The analysis focused on the dynamics of interactions between people and not on individual perceptions. In both organizations, the interactions took place in a staff meeting and consisted of intersubjective dialogue between two or more people. The findings include four subthemes of a) shared leadership, b) participatory decision-making, c) respect for others, and d) practice transparency in communication. These are summarized in Table 6.

The Organization A employee staff meeting began with 12 employees in attendance and increased to 15 by the mid-point of the call. Of these, 6 were Partners. Twelve people were visible and 3 were not as a result of having connected by phone line rather than video link. The Organization B senior management staff meeting was held in the head office boardroom. Nine members were present including the Executive Assistant to the CEO who managed the logistics of the meeting.

Table 6

Theme 4: Relational Equality

Subtheme	Key findings
1. Shared leadership	The Chair rotates within the meeting
2. Participatory decision-making	Strive for group consensus
3. Respect for others	Ensuring all voices are heard
4. Transparency in communications	Decisions and their rationale are shared

Shared leadership. While a senior leader launched the meeting in both organizations, the chair was subsequently handed off to different people at various times. The handoff was to whoever was the team lead or subject-matter expert for the next agenda item. In Organization A, both Partners and Associates took the lead at various times and eventually returned to the person who had originally launched the meeting. In Organization A, this was a Partner and in Organization B it was the CEO. Had the observer not known the position of the person taking the lead, it would not have been evident.

Participatory decision-making. There was only one example of decision-making between the two organizations. True to his word, the CEO avoided making the final decision. He tabled an item on the agenda that had presumably been brought to his attention previously. He indicated to the person who had raised the issue to take the chair. The individual provided background for the item and then opened the floor for discussion. Each person spoke in turn. People did not interrupt one another and allowed the current speaker to finish their thoughts. The group self-managed their discussion until everyone's voice had been heard. Once perspectives had been exhausted, the CEO asked for a show of hands in favor and against the decision. He then asked the minority dissenters if they could live with the decision. This appeared to be a genuine question as people were given time to comment. The dissenters agreed to live with the decision and it carried.

Respect for others. During the Organization A meeting, no one was interrupted when they spoke, and there were discernible pauses between speakers. This allowed time for people to formulate their thoughts and speak when they were ready. There was no sense of rushing or urgency across the entire hour. The meeting opened with an invitation from the Chair for people to praise others for their work. In one example, one group had completed a major project over the weekend and others offered positive comments about the quality of the effort. In the Organization B meeting, people were also polite, although the long pauses between speakers were not as in evidence as they were in Organization A and there was occasionally some talking over each other when a discussion became animated. However, no offense appeared to be taken. In the interviews, people specifically commented on how collegial this group is to work with.

Transparency in communication. In the Organization A meeting, several decisions had been made at the Partner level prior to the meeting and were being communicated to the group. In each case, the presenting Partner indicated that the need for the item under discussion had originated from within the Associates. That is, the Partners were responding to requests made by Associates. The presenting Partners for these items also disclosed the background and rationale for the final decision. In the interviews, it was clarified that project teams pursue many of these items. A Partner or Associate might chair a team meeting or Partners might support the Associate Chair. For such structuring to function effectively, transparency becomes essential such that the leader in a given situation is sufficiently informed and aware of context.

In Organization B, the item tabled for decision-making, as discussed above under the subtheme of participatory decision-making, would normally not be discussed at a senior management meeting. In most organizations, it would typically be dealt with between the CEO and the Board Chair, with input from a Vice President whose area was being affected. However, this CEO was demonstrating his transparency and inclusivity by making it possible for his team to participate in the decision-making on this item.

Theme 5: Innovating Strategic Frameworks

Theme 5 continues the exploration of how collaborative leaders construct power, but does so through a different lens than has thus far been employed. Data for this theme were collected through a review of documented systems and structures and from comments made during the interviews. The findings offer both new insights about and confirming evidence for the leaders' constructions of power discussed in Themes 1 through 3. The documents are listed in Appendix C. Only findings that are related to constructions of power are discussed.

This theme begins with an overview of the significant characteristics of each of the participating organizations. This overview is then followed by a review of the key findings common to both organizations. In an effort to protect the anonymity of the participants, the documents have not been identified by their official name, and have not been quoted from directly. There are five findings in common that inform the strategic frameworks for these two organizations. They are: a) principles-centered, b) values-based, c) founded on collaboration, d) devolved leadership, and e) prioritizes doing social good. Each of the findings is supported by secondary findings, as summarized in Table 7.

Table 7

Theme 5: Innovating Strategic Frameworks

Subtheme	Key findings
1. Principle-centered	Sustainability
	Social justice
	Democracy
	Altruism
	Profitability

2. Values-based	Eight common core values
	Learning organizations
3. Founded on collaboration	Articulated framework for collaboration
	Collaboration as a primary developmental focus
4. Devolved leadership	Shared ownership
	Minimized hierarchy
	Transparency in communication
5. Doing social good is prioritized	Leave the world a better place
	Fund projects
	Inspire external others

Overview. The founders of Organization A referred to it as a *conscious corporation*, meaning that they aspired to be socially conscious about their impact on both human beings and on the environment. Documents stated that the organization was intentionally designed to be human-centered, principles-guided, values-based, and socially responsible. The conceptual framework founded on the principle of justice guided the work of Organization A. This framework also informed how compensation, ownership, and governance were structured. At its core, this organization was founded on the belief that a civilization based on self-interested competition is incapable of solving the increasingly complex problems that humanity faces; it is only through the collaboration of diverse individuals and organizations that civilizations will find the best paths forward.

Organization B is a member-owned cooperative. The corporate website listed the specific criteria for cooperative enterprises. These were also found on the website for the International Co-operative Alliance (see Appendix H). There appeared to be an unstated belief that economic activity in the form of a business enterprise can add value to the earth and its people. To this end, Organization B backed up this belief by making explicit their commitment to sustainability. They also took direct action such as conducting supply chain audits for social and environmental performance, contributing a portion of their earnings to environmental concerns, and promoting the health and well-being of others. These others included, but were not limited to, employees, suppliers' employees, customers, and potential customers. The organization also aspired to serve as an example that inspires other people and organizations to support the goals and values of sustainability.

Principle-centered. The five principles that these organizations hold in common are the importance of sustainability, social justice, democratically inspired structures, and altruism.

Profitability is important for organization sustainability, but is secondary to the social goals. In terms of sustainability, both organizations speak to the complex social and ecological challenges facing humanity, and are seeking ways that their organizations can help to address them. The documents discuss their respective emphases on sustainability in some detail, including a variety of actions that range from conducting supply chain audits of social and environmental performance to funding projects that support social causes.

Social justice was specifically discussed by one organization from the perspective of being a foundational principle and was implied by the other. Justice refers to fairness and equity for the entire organization and was measured by the equitable distribution of wealth. Shared ownership models and direct actions substantiated the importance of social justice. The shared ownership models are discussed below. Examples of actions were social audits of the salaries, benefits, and working hours of Organization B's suppliers. A social audit is a means to evaluating for the purposes of improving an organization's social and ethical performance. Organization B committed to sever relationships if agreed-upon standards were not met and had already done so in at least one instance. This organization also provided a hotline for the employees within their supply chain to register concerns and complaints from anywhere in the world.

Democracy was at the core of both organizations. One organization indicated that its governance model for decision-making was designed to be democratic, and the other organization chose to function under democratic principles as part of its corporate charter. Altruism was also at the heart of both companies. The leaders of one believed that achieving their goals required that employees hold the capacity for altruistic service. Their underlying belief was that humans are as capable of learning and manifesting cooperation and altruism as they are opposite behaviors. To achieve this, the leaders endeavored to create an internal environment conducive to the expression of such behaviors. This organization also stood for the pursuit of excellence, innovation, and productivity in support of the greater good. The intention was to appeal to a fundamental human desire to serve a higher purpose in life. The second organization indirectly indicated the importance of altruism through its commitments to ethical practices, social justice, and specific corporate sustainability goals that target improving the environment.

Profitability was considered necessary rather than a central purpose. One organization is a charter member of a community of practice whose purpose is to learn about conducting business in new and responsible ways, while being in service to the common good. The greatest aspiration of the leaders of this organization was to create businesses that are just and sustainable and lead to shared human prosperity. A fundamental belief that these organizations held in common was that economic activity can and should leave both people and the environment in an improved state. While profitability is necessary to sustain and grow the business, they believe that need not be a primary goal. They viewed revenues as a means to sustain the enterprise.

Values-based. Both organizations had well-articulated core values and considered themselves to be learning organizations. Each organization listed nine core values, eight of which are common to both. While different terms are used, in most cases there was a similarity of intent. The nine common values are listed in Table 8. They are arranged in alphabetical order in column A and aligned by comparable values in column B.

Both of these organizations were considered by their members to be learning organizations. Senge (1990) coined the term learning organization to mean an organization "where people continually expand their capacity to create the results they truly desire, where new and expansive patterns of thinking are nurtured, where collective aspiration is set free, and where people are continually learning how to learn together" (p. 3). The leaders of one organization anticipated that people would need to remain in a continuous learning mode, recognizing that their development framework was complex and required a long-term commitment.

Table 8

Common Core Values

Column A	Column B
Balance Adventure	Collaboration
Cooperation	Common good
Humanity Discipline	Quality
Impact Stewardship	Integrity
Integrity Leadership	Leadership
Musing	Creativity

Note: While the value of collaboration is not listed here for the organization represented by Column B, it is included as one of their leadership competencies.

Both organizations maintained a mode of continuous improvement, reviewing their processes on a regular basis. They also applied methods such as Systems Mapping[9] and Lean[10] in order to identify the most effective and efficient means of conducting business.

Founded on collaboration. There are several secondary findings that shed light on the importance of collaboration to these organizations. Organization A designed a framework for collaboration that is intended to guide how they work together and further committed to reflect on their processes against this framework. For this organization, collaboration also represents a development focus. The core values in column A also represent the primary capacities for collaboration for that organization. Each of these collaboration capacities is further defined by values-based capacities presented in Appendix F. Employees were evaluated annually through a process that includes a multirater evaluation known more commonly as a 360-degree assessment. This evaluation took into consideration three aspects: level of capacity development, skill development, and performance against objectives. This same organization commissioned a literature review on collaboration to more fully understand the state of current knowledge for that subject and committed to regularly review all policies and practices against new understanding, as their practice of collaboration advanced.

Although collaboration is listed as a leadership competency within Organization B's Leadership Mastery program (see Appendix I), and the organization is founded on collaborative principles that underpin a cooperative model of governance, this organization has not invested extensive resources on formally developing collaborative capacity within its employees.

However, that may be changing. During the course of the

interviews for this study, Organization B was also working with a consulting firm to custom design a collaboration process for the senior leadership team. The purpose of this process was to ensure that issues would be dealt with in a similar and equally comprehensive manner. The process would be applied to projects where focused on creating new value as well as to complex challenges. Several of the participants who were interviewed after an offsite with the consulting firm where the collaboration process was launched expressed a desire to implement a similar approach within their team. One of the central concerns of this process was individual capacity to collaborate.

Devolved leadership. Three findings of shared ownership, minimized hierarchy, and transparency in communication emerged from the data. One organization intentionally chose to structure itself as a partnership precisely because this model aligns with its strategic framework and the notion of shared prosperity. The model included share distribution to all employees as part of the compensation program. The other organization is a member-owned cooperative, which is a form of devolved leadership. The CEO viewed his role to be a facilitator of decision- making within the senior leadership team.

Both organizations chose to minimize hierarchy and maintain the flattest possible structures. They conceived of hierarchy more as a differentiation in terms of scope of responsibility.

They also practiced transparency in communication. For example, one organization shared the Minutes of Partner meetings with the entire staff by posting them on the company intranet. The Partners also encouraged comments and questions about the Minutes. To reinforce this openness, they held weekly calls with all staff to cross communication decisions and project status. The CEO of the second organization maintained a blog where people could communicate directly with him. He also visited all company locations annually to meet with all staff. During these visits he held open forums and invited questions. No questions were considered out of bounds and he gave responses to all, even if the answer was that the issue being raised by the employee was not a priority for the company at this time.

Doing social good. The primary finding for this subtheme is that both organizations elevated the importance of doing social good. This finding is further defined by three goals: leave the world better than they found it, fund social and environmental projects, and inspire others external to the organization. Both organizations believed that industry and commerce could leave a positive footprint rather than have a detrimental effect on the world. Sustainability efforts and the focus on social justice described above are examples of this orientation. Both organizations annually set aside a percentage of revenues for purposes of funding causes and projects that align with their stated goals and purpose.

Theme 6: Shaping the Environment

Theme 6 emerges out of the interview data. It explores leader intentions and actions as they pertain to constructions of power. As a reminder, the construction of a concept requires both thought and action to be fully constituted. Theme 6 considers leader actions in terms of how they sustain or intend to sustain their constructions of power through shaping the environment. Three subthemes emerged from the data: a) leadership practices, b) character, and c) culture and are further parsed into key findings. Theme 6 is summarized in Table 9.

Table 9

Theme 6: Shaping the Environment

Subtheme	Key findings
1. Leadership practices	Consulting others
	Participatory decision-making
	Working through conflict
	Putting others ahead of self
	Promoting relational equality
	Valuing diversity
	Transparency in communication
2. Character	Humility
	Trustworthiness and trust
	Courage
3. Culture	Creates a supportive culture
	Develops a learning organization
	Ensures the environment feels safe

The first subtheme, leadership practices, sheds light on the participants' preferred approaches to enacting leadership. The second subtheme of character represents how the participants comported themselves. The third and final subtheme of culture offers a perspective on how leaders engaged at a systems level. Together, these findings further illuminate the thoughts and actions that inform a collaborative leader's constructions of power, and the environment they shape to sustain those constructions.

Leadership practices. This subtheme offers insight into how the participants acted on their thoughts and beliefs about mutualistic power. It does so by exploring the leadership practices they most frequently discussed in the interviews. Leadership practices are defined in various ways in the literature. This will be explored in greater detail in Chapter 5. At this juncture, suffice to say that they represent the intentions of the participants in terms of leading others. There are seven practices of consulting others, participatory decision-making, working through conflict, putting others ahead of self, promoting relational equality, valuing diversity, and practicing transparency in their communication. Each of these findings is further parsed into secondary findings, as summarized in Table 10.

Consulting others. Twenty-one of 25 participants mentioned the importance of consultation as an essential element of their decision-making process. As decision-making is a core expression of power, understanding how collaborative leaders make decisions sheds light on how they enact power. In this study, to consult means to confer with others prior to making a decision. The three secondary findings are that consultation improves buy-in and ownership of decisions, consultation improves decision and implementation quality, and conflict is an expected part of consultative conversations.

Kolten stated that collaborative leadership "draws its truth from a synthesis of the collective. I think that collaborative leadership is a leadership that allows for input prior to decisions, critique after decisions, and necessitates the humility to course correct." These leaders frequently consulted with stakeholders prior to making decisions and communicated their decisions once made. The consensus view was that there are distinct advantages to this approach.

Table 10

Subtheme 1: Leadership Practices

Key findings	Secondary findings
1. Consulting others	Consultation improves buy-in and ownership of decisions
	Consultation improves decision and implementation quality
	Conflict can emerge in consultative conversations
2. Participatory decision-making	Collaborative decision-making captures a diversity of perspectives
	Collaborative decision-making promotes group unity and trust
	Collaborative decision-making can be at the expense of efficiency
3. Working through conflict	Working through conflict is a learned skill
4. Putting others ahead of self	Collaborative leaders demonstrate a high level of selflessness
	Collaborative leaders work in service to others
5. Promoting relational equality	Collaborative leaders view followers as complementary and commensurate
6. Valuing diversity	Having a variety of viewpoints is important for decision-making
	The reasons for including a variety of perspectives vary
7. Transparency in communication	People need more information to be able to collaborate effectively
	The importance of communications permeates organizational boundaries out into the larger environment

The most frequently stated advantage to consulting others is that it improves buy-in to and ownership of decisions. Nerita said, "If a decision is made collaboratively, or at least it's been discussed with a bigger group, you generally tend to have more buy-in from those that were involved in creating the decision." Frank remarked, "I'll get a much better buy-in if I include people in the solution." The decisions themselves are viewed to be of a higher quality, largely because multiple perspectives are first considered. Robert said, "We'll make better decisions if we're engaging others in the company as well." And Rachel commented that "you've used everyone's best insights, their best thoughts . . . you've pulled their brains into it basically."

The implementation of decisions was also seen to be of a higher quality. In this regard, Benjamin said, "I think everyone feels more connected to the decisions that are made and more supportive of them . . . people work more intently toward that goal because they really got to that place with you." And Margaret observed,

> Overall, you will get . . . a better organizational result. People will be happier. People much prefer being part of something than being told what to do, and so, therefore, you get more by it, and hopefully, people work harder, and people are more aligned in the work that they're doing. It's definitely a more comfortable place to be.

Consultative conversations were not represented as calm easy-going conversations; conflict can and does emerge and is to be expected. Rosemary observed that

> there needs to be dialogue and discussions and disagreements in order for, at the end of the day, at the end of the meeting, you have collaborated to a point where you've heard people's concerns, you've heard people's disagreements . . . issues are brought to the

table and you're forced to discuss them.

Participatory decision-making. All participants discussed the importance of collaborative decision-making. Collaborative decision-making means that decisions are made by two or more people collectively, as distinct from consultation where one person makes a final decision after consulting with others. The three secondary findings are that collaborative decision-making (a) captures a diversity of perspectives, (b) promotes group unity and trust, and (c) can be at the expense of efficiency.

In general, these leaders had a clear preference for making decisions in a collaborative manner, partly because it enabled them to bring together a diversity of perspectives. Bryce stated, "when you reach this level you know that you can't act alone." He went on to explain that "you form a group and then that group has a defined process and different roles, and everybody knows their role, and then we make that decision together." Hannah believed "it is achieving whatever it is you want to achieve, the result that is, but doing it through as many functional areas or organizations or bringing in as many stakeholders, partners as you can to get the best result." In a similar vein, Tyrone explained that

> nobody can be a subject matter expert on everything. And nobody can have all the answers to every big decision that's made. We live in an increasing state of complexity, and while we all require a big picture view and that's important. Just to sit at an executive table and to have that—it's important to trust people in different areas of expertise.

Participants stated that the process of collaborative decision-making promotes group unity and trust. As identified elsewhere, trust appeared to be an important factor for the success of collaborative leadership. Selma said,

> I think that you want people to unify and once again to feel that there is some democracy that people have a voice. That people are not just demanded to do something. I think when you do collaborate I think there is trust in the process that says that your opinion counts.

Dorothy observed, "We need to trust people where they have experience in different places, different backgrounds, so we put that together and get to a better place."

While some potential downsides to collaborative decisonmaking were expressed, the general view is that challenges can be resolved over time as the individuals and groups become more proficient in the process. Farren reflected,

> We're trying to be highly collaborative but any time you're highly collaborative on decision-making you obviously lose efficiency. And in some cases you don't end up with a better outcome other than people might be happy that they're involved. So I still think we're sorting that out.

Working through conflict. Ten of 12 participants in Organization A indicated that they were beginning to deal well with conflict, although they viewed it as a learning process. The most frequently cited approach was to talk through the conflict. That occurred in one-on-one conversations or when mediated by a third party.

In Organization A, senior leaders encouraged conflicting parties to speak directly to one another and intervened only when that process failed. Kolten said, "We actually really encourage . . . people to speak directly with each other." Farren explained the challenges of dealing with conflict in a virtual environment, particularly when relationships were relatively new. She said,

> We also recognize that there are times, especially in newer relationships and we're virtual, so that really compounds I think the ability to really work through conflict because you can't see people on a day-to-day basis. And if you don't know people, if you don't have that relationship, it's just hard and it's something that we're learning quite a bit about. You know the speed of trust is greatly diminished in a completely virtual environment so there are times when people escalate to partners. And then we sit down and have conversations and try to understand you know, where the conflict's coming from? What are people's different opinions, thoughts, etc?

Comments from Organization B participants indicated less directedness in dealing with conflict, and a recognition that they needed to improve in this area. Selma said she encourages people to talk together "and work it through," and Bryce believed this is the approach they should be using. A few participants, such as Malcolm, suggested that they could be candid and direct and prefer to address issues immediately. The majority of the Organization B participants indicated that while there has been some definite growth in this area, there is some room for improvement. As a consequence, they were experiencing some conflict avoidance and recognized that this state of affairs is not positive for effective collaboration. For example, Rachel observed,

> I still think there's hesitation to like constructively challenge some, you know, someone else's area and then they might be defensive about that. So I think that's the dynamic that goes on that we still need to work through and improve.

Frank commented in a similar fashion when he said, "And, certainly, we have individuals that are getting better at that. But, yeah, we sort of have some way to go on that."

A distinguishing factor between Organizations A and B was that the former provided conflict mediation training to the organizational members by tapping into the expertise of one of their Associates. This action ensures that everyone has a basic understanding of how to recognize and address conflict when it arises and a framework to work with toward conflict resolution. By contrast, Organization B has not yet identified a formal process.

Putting others ahead of self. Sixteen of 25 participants made comments about the importance of leaders putting others ahead of themselves. The two secondary findings are that collaborative leaders demonstrate a high level of selflessness, and collaborative leaders work in service to others. Participants reported that they demonstrate a high level of interest in others and in the organization and less for themselves. Garth said,

> There's a lot less self-interest involved in collaborative leadership. We're all trying to put the organization and put each other first as opposed to maybe putting personal goals first that you kind of see in a traditional leadership structure.

Farren self-reported, "The purpose is to bring whatever I have to share and then just—and to— it's almost to kind of give it as an offering and try to do what you think is really important." Tyrone reinforced this view by saying, "it's not about me, this is about the organization."

> Margaret also shared that one of the things that I really love about [Organization B] is that there's very little ego involved in decision-making, and there's, I think, pretty

much universally, the people I see making decisions and leveraging their power are doing it because they think it's ultimately in the best interests of the organization and its membership.

A significant focus for participants was the development of potential. They endeavored to achieve this through being of service to others. Henry said, "I think the collaborative leadership is sort of really coming from that space and seeing one another as human beings and then cultivating—creating an environment, enabling environment so that we can reach our full potential." Dexter observed that there is "a sincere wish to help everybody else excel and be successful." Robert concurred when he contributed, "I think there's this element of service that's a part of it." And Benjamin stated that

> when you're managing people it's more about working with folks as individuals and helping them grow for their own sake, grow for the company's sake and grow for the sake of the impact of the work they're trying to have. I think that being a manager to people is really about serving those people. If I'm a good manager that means that I am serving them by supporting them . . . I am essentially extending the impact that I can have on the world by building up the ability for others to have that impact.

Alongside this selflessness and intention of being in service was a concomitant sense of promoting relational equality by leaders not elevating themselves above their followers. Lawrence said, "I never think of myself as a great leader. I think of myself as part of a strong team." And Henry noted, "I don't think people or the partners observe in their minds thinking they are higher or superior."

Promoting relational equality. Fourteen of 25 participants discussed some aspect of how equality is important to them. The secondary findings indicate that collaborative leaders viewed followers as complementary and commensurate. Henry said,

> There's that sense of seeing one another as human beings. Yes, we will have different skills and different experiences and different stages of development, some are more similar and more experienced than the other but fundamentally we are the same as human beings and so respecting and loving one another at that level and then tapping into that deeper source of what is it that we want to cocreate together.

Nala described collaborative leadership as

> that sharing of influence or power or control or whatever we call it; it's sharing decision-making; sharing the outcomes of decisions as well; in an environment that's more consultative, not competitive. And also where the roles are complementary. Not necessarily equal but complementary.

While the leaders had a greater scope of responsibility when compared to their followers, they did not view themselves, and were not viewed by others, as being more important or better than others. They were valued and respected for their knowledge, experience, and scope of responsibility that they carried in their respective roles. Dexter exemplified this when he said, "leadership is definitely one of being part of the group, so it's not as if I am the—you never feel a 'I am the partner and therefore...' You really feel the partner's totally at the same level."

From the perspective of the CEO, Lawrence reinforced this notion of equality when he said,

I really do hire people that know more than I do, and my team is a team of people that think differently to the way I do; their skills in what they do are greater than mine. So it's my job to set the direction and then let everyone loose and let them do what they're best at doing.

Promoting relational equality underlined and supported having a diversity of perspectives in decision-making.

Valuing diversity. Fifteen of 25 participants spoke of the value of diversity in decision- making. Secondary findings show the importance of including a variety of viewpoints in decision-making, and the reasons for seeking a diversity of perspectives vary.

Bryce used the metaphor of a hockey team, explaining that a team needs a variety of skills, but that the skills need to be complementary. He stated, "Not one person can have the depth for all the skills, so you need to have a team." Hannah observed that diversity can also mean people are honest and will speak the truth to leaders; they cannot be yes men. Selma and Rosemary commented that it is incumbent upon leaders to seek out input. Selma said leaders must use their "capabilities to get everybody to discuss the issue at hand" and that "you always make sure that you take in all your stakeholders. You make sure that you make people, interested parties, feel like they do have a say."

The reason why a diversity of perspectives was important to leaders varied. Lawrence stated that diversity provides the critical voice that keeps the team on task and makes it stronger. He said, "You get a much better result, and a much more creative outcome." Dorothy said,

> the best solution will come out of bringing diverse ideas together and being able to debate and nurture that diversity so that we can come up with something

even better. So that it's a way of, yeah, getting to a better place and being able to create more creatively, solve problems or be able to take advantage of new opportunities, adding value to the organization.

Nerita complemented this perspective when she stated,

> I think ultimately because you're gaining more perspectives, you hopefully get to better conclusions because you're not just looking at the perspective of a few people… I find that when everybody is included you're able to get a more
>
> holistic understanding and perspective.

There were challenges associated with having multiple viewpoints. As Lawrence noted, "It can get a little bit messy at times." Malcolm commented that it could also take more time because one needs to reach out to more people. Dorothy exemplified this perspective with a brief story of mentoring one of her team members.

> I had this discussion with someone on my team who's been a little frustrated with the more collaborative process, because she's very much a driver and wants to get things done. And in her past she's seen organizations where one person just makes all the decisions and then it's gone, right, and it's out and it's been done. So from her perspective, it's more efficient and she doesn't have to wait for other people.
>
> She knows what she wants; she just wants to get it done. But on the collaborative side, there's a little bit of a slowing down at the beginning as you bring in the diversity of opinions, but then it's a decision and then you are off with better input, and better decision-making if it's done well. So it's more . . . I've been working with

her to explain this is the value that you're getting from it and we need to build in some time, and as we do this more often it'll become quicker and you won't feel like it's been slowed down. Ultimately, we need to trust people where they have experience in different places, different backgrounds, so we put that together and get to a better place.

Transparency in communication. Nineteen participants of 25 spoke of the importance of communication in collaborative organizations. This is not surprising given that collaborative decision-making requires knowledge of what is occurring within the organization. The secondary findings show that people need more information to be able to collaborate effectively, and that the importance of communication permeates organizational boundaries out into the larger environment.

Samantha explained that

> collaborative leadership would involve more availability of information across an organization so that the right people could make the decisions that are relevant to them and in an efficient way without necessarily having to go up a hierarchy or through, kind of, a narrowing process up to, let's say, the peak of the pyramid and then back down. Which can be a big bottleneck, as we've seen sometimes.

Patricia mirrored this view when she offered the following example:

> [My manager] always brings us into his decisions or what he's working on right now and just talks it through with us, even if it's not something that I might be directly working on, but just to kind of bring me up to speed and make sure I'm aware of all the big things that are going on and then even just as a learning opportunity for me,

he'll just talk me through what he might be doing.

Rachel reinforced the importance of communication, particularly where there were decisions that had been made collaboratively by the senior management team.

> I think as a leader, as an organization if you're going to go out and explain a decision to your staff that maybe is controversial . . . or just a new strategic direction, I think you want to have the benefit of being able to explain like what was the dialogue at the table and like what were the pros and cons and why did we head this way. And I think it's just, I think it will better inform the entire organization.

As CEO, Lawrence viewed communication as one of his top three responsibilities. He commented that he needs to be "communicating and telling stories about the future so that the culture can move to that desired place."

The importance of communication extended beyond the organization and out into interactions with clients. Samantha described the conference calls she hosted in her role as Engagement Manager. The project extended to volunteers around the globe. She said,

> I have the information that I need to, sort of, communicate to them but I also have the opportunity to work directly with all of those people and support them in that process of understanding, digesting that information and then executing on it at the local level. It's an opportunity for me to share a whole bunch of information with them; invite them to ask questions; to respond directly to their questions, you know, personally, verbally on the phone; and, to let everyone else hear the responses and so, to understand and benefit from that information as well.

It is important to note that this level of communication was not always in evidence. Nala observed that "it's taken some time to have a communication flow that has been steady and reliable coming from the partnership to the rest of the company." The need for communication was something that had been recognized and addressed over time. As Tyrone pointed out, communicating can be more important than actually making a decision. He explained that

> it could be more inclusive in a longer way.... And that's often what it's about, it's about like, you do have, you know, you do have a stake in this and I just want to let you know that I'm recognizing you have a stake in this. Which is as important as, you know, that recognition is often as important as the decision itself.

Rosemary noted the consequences of insufficient communication. She said,

> I think we waste a lot of time doing that sometimes. Rather than, "We're in this meeting to make decisions, let's bring up all the issues, let's leave the meeting with: here are the outcomes of the meeting, here's the strategy leaving the meeting, and let's start working on it immediately," I think we waste a lot of time between the meeting and actually putting things into motion because there's not enough dialogue in the actual meeting.

Dorothy said that insufficient communication can lead to conflict:

> Sometimes it stems from people being really busy and a lack of communication, so there's frustration because they haven't had a chance to debate things or, you know, decisions are being made without you at the table.

Character. Three primary findings for character emerged

from the data. These are (a) humility, (b) trustworthiness and trust, and (c) courage. Collectively, they represent the most frequently cited character traits. Each of these findings is further broken down into secondary findings as summarized in Table 11.

Humility. Twenty-four of 25 participants made at least one comment, and in many cases several comments, that indicated the importance of a collaborative leader demonstrating humility. Participant responses to questions demonstrated a high level of humility in general. This was reflected in their willingness to be open about where they were not perfect, where they experienced challenges, and where they were applying their learning to be more effective.

Table 11

Subtheme 2: Character

Key findings	Secondary findings
1. Humility	Leaders endeavor to minimize ego
	Leaders are self-reflective and try to be honest with themselves
2. Trustworthiness and trust	Trust and trustworthiness are fundamental to collaborative leadership
	The absence or loss of trust has negative consequences
3. Courage	Sometimes collaborative leaders need to stand alone
	Courageous stands are in the interests of the greater good

The secondary findings suggest that these leaders endeavor to minimize their ego, and they are self-reflective and try to be honest with themselves. Farren spoke about how she brings herself to her work when she said,

> The purpose is to bring whatever I have to share and then just . . . it's almost to kind of give it as an offering and try to do what you think is really important but yet at the end of the day you don't own it.

Henry observed that "when the environment does not respond well to my intervention, I realize the limitation of my power and then choose a different course of exercising my power." Robert said, "I think it makes me feel good, on one hand, but also it makes me really question, like I can't become complacent as well, thinking okay I did this now I'm okay."

Many of these leaders indicated that they reflect on their leadership. For example, Samantha talked about her project where she was responsible for coordinating teams of people around the globe over whom she had no formal authority. She was experiencing a challenge with one group in particular, where circumstances had required her to guide them somewhat more forcefully than would otherwise be desirable. She lamented that

> at the moment, none of them are very happy with me and so, I don't think I'm doing it well. So, I think, that's a good example in which I'm not exercising power well, though I haven't figured how yet to improve it.

Lawrence also demonstrated this self-reflective nature when he openly reported on his past transgressions. He commented,

> We're always right in our own minds, aren't we? I know that I have been clumsy and careless in the past and I know that I have done things in the past because I hadn't understood the implications of power. And what I mean

by that is that in assuming a role of leadership, I think very often you don't understand what that leadership means to people around you and beneath you, and what the assumption of that role of authority is.

Selma suggested that such humility attracts people. She explained that "a powerful person can admit their mistakes, can turn and say, 'That decision I made was wrong,' or 'We should have done a hybrid of that' or something like that. And people will still admire them."

Trustworthiness and trust. Eighteen of 25 participants used the word *trustworthiness* or a stem word such as *trust* in 80 instances throughout the interviews. They stated that trustworthiness and trust are fundamental to collaborative leadership and therefore to constructions of power, and that the absence or loss of trust has negative consequences. Everyone being trustworthy enables collaborative decision-making, aids in resolving conflicts, and supports leaders in their efforts to guide and influence followers. These three areas were also considered to be the ones where power is most likely to be used. Being trustworthy enables open dialogue and getting honest feedback.

Malcolm stated, "in terms of making decisions, I would say that the first word that jumps to mind is trust." Dexter observed, "People really trust the leadership in a way that I've seen in very few other companies." He continued by saying,

> You really trust everybody else to step up, to give it their best, really perform in a great way, so there's a level of trust, and you trust that each person that's responsible for something will actually do it to their best capacity.... And obviously in the communication as well so trust that people will communicate in an open, transparent way without hiding anything else and really giving the

facts as they are.

Robert shared these same sentiments, particularly as they relate to getting honest feedback. He said,

> I think that, at least one of the things in the company that we talk about a lot is how—and this is true for myself and I've certainly seen it—we don't have a mirror, we can't see ourselves, we rely on others to help ourselves see ourselves. And so it's about how can you have trusted people around you who love you, care for you, who could actually give you that feedback, even if you may not want to hear it.

Trust was considered central to resolving and avoiding conflict. Benjamin offered to any team member who was experiencing conflict with another the following advice:

> If we're going to resolve this conflict, you need to come with the intention for trust and resolution and openness. That's where you have to come to the table or else it's going to be far more painful than it needs to be.

He also shared how he tried to mitigate conflict arising by asking them to take one another at face value. He explained,

> I guess I want to get people to the point where they—and I'm realizing the challenges but one thing I've been trying is getting people to the point where they can take what someone is saying at face value and as the truth and operate on that base assumption of trust.

Tyrone noted the importance of trust building for effective decision-making. He stated that

> the individual trust between managers can't… be overstated. That is critical as is building up the trust within the team, and I don't think any amount of sort of, corporate exercise that really make, you know, team

building exercises. It's more what you bring—your own kind of personal brand and if you do that, and you know, conduct yourself in that sort of confident but open and honest sort of thing, the trust builds and you're in a far better place to make decisions.

He said that by building trusting relationships with one's peers it is easier to gain a better perspective of the other person's organization, and one can therefore give appropriate consideration to how decisions will impact that organization.

Malcolm exemplified how trust and trustworthiness combine. He talked about the importance of his own behavior and how it impacted the openness of communication between himself and his managers:

For me, the level of trust I think starts with how I behave, because I think I build the trust by how I react to various situations and circumstances for my store managers, the store management teams. Because everything they do with me in terms of building trust and confiding and being transparent all has to deal with how I react to what they tell me. So if their business is bad or if they had a bad situation in the store and I jump all over them or threaten them, I'm going to break down that level of trust.

Dorothy noted, "once there's trust and respect, that helps; it's the foundation for the collaboration." When Frank compared traditional leadership to collaborative leadership he observed, "one of the key distinctions is trust through the whole group."

As with all things, there is a shadow side to trust. Several participants cautioned that when trust is not in evidence, or breaks down, it erodes people's ability to maintain the relationships that are central to collaborative leadership and therefore mutualistic power.

Rosemary told the story of a new CEO who built and subsequently eroded the trust within the organization. The net result was utter chaos. Hannah cautioned that when trust has been eroded it takes a long time to rebuild it, and sometimes it cannot be rebuilt. When asked if she had repaired a relationship damaged by her own behavior, she replied,

> I did, I tried. It took about, you've eroded that trust. It takes a long time to get it back. I, yeah eventually probably got three quarters of it back but never got it to where it should've been. In my mind, right? Maybe I'm over-exaggerating but I don't know, that's how it always felt to me. It always felt like there was always that element of, not distrust but just like questioning my judgement.

Courage. While there is a clear sense in the data that collaborative leaders believed they needed to act in partnership with others, many explained that there are times that they needed to stand apart. The secondary findings for courage show that sometimes, collaborative leaders need to stand alone, and courageous stands are in the interests of the greater good. Thirteen of 25 participants shared stories of leadership courage as an important use of power. The stories participants shared fall into three categories.

The first category is comprised of stories about the participants themselves. Nala reported an incident where she openly challenged a leader who was engaging in theft of corporate property.

> I had to say "You can't do this. You can't abuse this privilege. It's also against the law." And I thought maybe I made one enemy but I also really engendered the trust of a group of 20 people in the field. And I felt like I really upheld the principles that I was supposed to. But it was

a hard decision.

Tyrone talked about an occasion where he refused to exaggerate an insurance claim as requested by his client. He continued by discussing the need to take a stand.

> I think that as a leader, it's easy to stand together; it's easy to stand together as a group and support your team. It's a lot harder to stand alone. When you're convinced that you're right and not everybody else is, but you've got to go back to what you believe your role is and what you believe . . . what's best for the organization. And, ultimately, if you are making that decision in your heart of hearts, and with what you believe is right for the organization, a very strong leadership quality is the ability to stand alone and to bring people to cross that divide between . . . where they are and where you are.

The second category is composed of stories of leaders that the participants had worked with at some point in their careers. Hannah spoke of a CEO at the country level who held a vision for a novel approach to merchandizing that took several years to successfully sell within the international organization:

> It took seven years to get that store open and she would, she presented the business case, got shot down, presented the business case differently, shot down, then she started to try. . . she tried the front door, the back door, the window to try and get it and she thought I'll go through the basement window. She tried different, a different approach using her power but pulling in different examples, different stakeholders to get a project approved.

Once implemented, the idea was so successful that it ultimately became a cornerstone concept within the larger corporation. Farren shared the story of a CEO who committed to, and achieved, a vision of sourcing conflict-free materials for the company's manufacturing process. Carl talked about how his current CEO pushed against the resistance of the senior leadership team to engage suppliers in a dialogue about social audits. The project went ahead and proved to be a great success. It was a particular success with the suppliers because they had wondered if anyone actually cared about their efforts, as no one had ever asked.

The third category consists of stories about leaders the participants did not know but had read, or heard, stories about. For example, Holly talked about Ray Anderson, the founder and former CEO and Chairman of Interface Inc. Anderson was a pioneer in introducing the concept of sustainability into industry and encouraged other major corporations to follow suit. Lawrence spoke of the graceful power of Nelson Mandela in assuming the leadership of South Africa and the equally graceful power of F. W. de Klerk in releasing power to Mandela.

The courageous stand that each of the leaders in these examples took was always in the interests of the greater good. Not only were they unselfishly motivated, in a few instances the leaders put their career and/or credibility at risk. It is also notable that many participants recalled stories where leaders challenged cultural norms. On reflection, one can see that many of these leaders ultimately made significant contributions to a shift in thinking beyond their own organization and out into the external culture. Such stories speak to the combined use of courage and power and to the high ethical standards that collaborative leaders appear to hold themselves to. Lawrence specifically named courage as one of the most important attributes a leader needs in terms of using power. He said, "I'm looking at good power in this case, and to me that's two things: the one is knowledge and the other one is courage."

There are three additional categories mentioned by many of the study participants, but by fewer than 50%. These are self-awareness, respect for others, and patience. No specific questions were designed to evoke thoughts on the importance of character; those shared here were voluntarily offered. Had there been a question, based on how participants responded to similar questions, it is anticipated that the majority would also have mentioned these last three aspects of character. Additionally, in an earlier study of collaborative leaders (Davis, 2013), these same character traits were discussed by the majority of participants.

Culture. While an exploration of organizational culture was not an intended part of the study, many of the participants made comments about their respective organizational cultures that shed light on how power is conceived of. Three findings of note are that the leaders (a) create a supportive culture, (b) develop a learning organization, and (c) ensure the environment feels safe. Each of these findings is further expanded into a second level of findings, as summarized in Table 12.

Creates a supportive culture. Seventeen of 25 participants commented about their organizational culture. At a summary level, the comments support the secondary finding that these cultures are happy and inclusive. Garth observed, "There's a strong level of attachment to the organization that you don't see too often or at least you don't hear about too often. And everybody does seem to be very happy in their role." Bryce said, "Every company is different in culture and style of leadership, and I've been in quite a few and this is by far the best one as far as culture." Hannah described Organization B as "a very nice happy organization" where "everybody's happy and friendly and everybody wants to get along. So it's, there's not, yeah it's different."

Table 12

Subtheme 3: Culture

Key findings	Secondary findings
1. Creates a supportive culture	Cultures are happy and inclusive
2. Develops a learning organization	The organizations are becoming learning organizations; it is a process
	Much of the learning is around decision-making processes
3. Ensures the environment feels safe	People feel safe to speak freely and candidly without recourse

Selma explained the importance of maintaining a postive culture. She stated that

> in our culture we want people to believe that this is their company too. That they are part and parcel of the success of the organization. And I think when you do that, when you explain things, when you ask for opinions, when you have an open dialogue with your staff—our CEO does a blog, people answer it, ask questions. I think when you collaborate like that with people, I think that there is a feel about the organization that is very positive. It can be very positive.

Carl commented that

> by virtue of the way [Organization B] operates, it draws a certain type of person that is principled, wants some work life balance, really values being able to lead an active lifestyle but, as well, do really meaningful work and work really hard.

And, Frank noted, "the cool thing about [Organization B] is there's just always opportunity here and I'm not really sure why. It might be because of the passion of the staff and how they believe so strongly in the organization" and that "there's a lot of pride in [Organization B]. They belong here . . . they come here because they believe that they're working for an organization that believes in people, that believes in doing things a different way."

Develops a learning organization. Seventeen of 25 participants commented on being a *learning organization*. Some participants specifically used this term, while others spoke more generally about the importance of learning for their organization. The secondary findings are that the organizations are becoming learning organizations; it is a process, and much of the learning is around decision-making processes.

Henry said, "It's a continuous process. I'm not saying we're able to get it right away. It's a continuous learning process and learning internally and also learning with our client system." Holly observed,

> We're very much a learning organization and we are still striving really hard to figure out how to do [collaboration], how to own it and how to tell the story. How to define it, so it's very much a work in progress because it's definitely not a – clearly it's not the dominant paradigm in the world. It's something we are striving to figure out how to do to good effect.

And, Lawrence said,

> We're getting better at learning. We weren't. I think that we were a fairly ossified organization; we've come a long way. The changes that we've effected since 2012 have been pretty dramatic. I believe we are becoming a very good learning organization, but we're not there yet.

Comments predominantly addressed learning about

collaborative decision-making. Participants referenced a variety of issues under this topic such as what it really means to be collaborative, how to make collaborative decisions, and finding the right balance between what needs to be consulted on at the organizational level and what does not. In a collaborative culture, it is important to sort out who needs to participate in what decisions. Both organizations have developed tools to aid in developing their decision-making processes. Organization A developed a decision-making matrix that considers who needs to be involved in what decisions, while Organization B took this a step further. They designed a process for bringing forward and working through issues of a strategic nature at the senior management level. Both organizations also employ familiar learning processes such as Systems Mapping, group offsites, facilitated workshops, Lean, and internal and external subject matter consultants.

Participants noted the challenges to learning. For example, Holly commented on the "inherent cultural elements that inform our attitudes and behaviors and I think a lot of them are very unconscious. I think they thwart our learning and our process because they get in the way of new behaviors." Lawrence observed, "one of the things that we have to crack is to stop this, or fight this desire to say 'but we've always done it that way and it served us well, we've always done it that way.'" He continued with:

> I think that very often you have to understand that there are some things that are very important to your organization and set you apart that you need to safeguard, and there are other practices—best practices or intuitive practices—that have been developed through systems and vendors, that you need to adapt to make you better. So what makes you different and where are you no different?

In terms of how important learning is to collaborative organizations, Lawrence illustrated this when he shared his inspiration from modern dance doyenne Martha Graham. He said, "we have to have a state of divine dissatisfaction, because we can never stop changing, we can never stop improving."

Ensures the environment feels safe. Almost 50% of the participants spoke about the importance of having a safe environment to support collaborative leadership. The central secondary finding is that with collaborative leadership, people feel safe to speak freely and candidly without recrimination.

The need for safety is understood at all levels of the organization. Kolten observed, "their relationship turned around because there was an open dialogue, a safe environment. And, there was no—nobody was reprimanded because of it in any way." Malcolm spoke in a similar vein when he stated that

> it's got to be a safe environment. It's easy to say "everybody share your thoughts," but people know if it's a safe environment or not. There has to be opportunity for challenging, for probing and for data, so I don't know if that answers your question or not. But collaborative means all parties have the opportunity to share their voice.

Carl further reinforced this when he observed, "It's a safe environment for people to table issues and their perspectives, without fear of repercussion." The adjectives that were most repeated by the participants to describe their safe environment were enabling, non-competitive, respectful, safe, supportive, and trusting. These align well with the adjectives participants used to describe collaborative leaders.

Contradictory Findings

Most of the data collected for this study suggest a high

level of integrity in terms of an alignment between intentions and actions to construct power in mutualistic terms. Comments were made by many of the participants that indicated their organization and their leaders were by no means perfect. However, there was no consistency to these comments across the participant group. Points of view were not shared across the employee group let alone across the two organizations. Points of view were generally localized in the individual. It should be remembered that the threshold for inclusion in the study was representation by at least 50% of the participants. Following are a few examples of the kinds of comments made by participants, followed by a discussion of the one area where some consistency was identified.

Occasionally, there were turns of phrases made by a participant that might raise doubt about whether he or she was consistently employing mutualistic power. For example, one participant talked about *allowing* people to develop their capacity, where allowing is the offending word. This turn of phrase might suggest that they viewed themselves as powerful and were sharing the power they possessed with others. However, I also noted that English was not this person's primary tongue and all of the other statements this participant made comport with a notion of mutualistic power. I specifically questioned the participant on this point and was satisfied that his response indicated a clear intent to draw out the capacity of followers rather than impart power to them. In another case, a participant commented on his frustrations with how the organization engaged in consultation and how he would prefer to just focus on his work rather than participate. This individual also expressed high ideals in terms of how consultation could function and felt that the organization was not living up to these ideals. This was a personalized concern.

In one of the organizations there had been a parting of

ways with two individuals. A few of the participants commented on these events. The leaders who had been involved in the decision-making talked about the long process they had gone through to try and salvage the situation. The associates who spoke of this talked about the thoroughness and comprehensive efforts that had been made to turn the situation around before the decision had been made to terminate relations. While the participants expressed sadness over these events, they also seemed to feel that all had been done that could be done.

However, one clear contradictory finding did emerge from the data. Followers continue to project power as dominance onto the leaders in spite of leader efforts to exercise mutualistic power. There was ample evidence in the interview data that followers perceived a difference in power between leaders and followers. Comments indicated that followers projected power onto their leaders. There is also evidence that leaders make clear efforts to minimize any power gap between themselves and their followers in hierarchically lower levels.

Excluding senior leaders, there were 19 participants in the study who are classified as followers by virtue of their reporting relationship. In Organization A, 7 report to partners and in Organization B, 12 report to the CEO. Of these 19, 10 contributed comments coded to this topic. While all study participants were considered to be leaders, there were hierarchical distinctions among the participants in both organizations. Organization A partners were the senior leaders of that organization, as was the CEO of Organization B. Comments made about these leaders by all other participants were segregated and evaluated.

Ross warns of the dangers of projection when he says, "your motivations might become more about pleasing that person. You might also start to deify or reify a particular individual which then limits how much of your capacity is expressed." Nerita believes a root cause of this distinction lies in how leaders and followers view reality. Each has distinctive perspectives about what is going on. Rather than seeing a need to change this distinction, she believes this challenge can be overcome through consultative decision-making. Because Organization A operates with such a high level of transparency, Dexter has witnessed firsthand follower behavior in response to the leaders. He observed what he interpreted as a few Associates seeking the approval of the Partners. When this approval was received, he believes it caused the Associates to seek even more approval.

Holly observed similar behavior. She said, "I do think within the organization there is a dynamic that is very conventional despite all of our efforts, and so behaviors may be different on group calls when a partner is involved." However, she believes the followers, rather than having been initiated or encouraged in any way by the partners, impose this dynamic. She senses "some kind of power dynamic that may not actually be there, but we impose even from the bottom up because we're in the room with someone perceived to have or actually does have more power." She believed that "there are inherent cultural elements that inform our attitudes and behaviors and I think a lot of them are unconscious. I think they thwart our learning and our process because they get in the way of new behaviors."

The resultant behavior is either that followers endeavor to impress the leader or engage in what she refers to as *dumbing down* an opinion expressed with greater passion when senior leaders are not present. She offered an example of power differentials at play when people do not respond to requests from a peer Associate. When a leader subsequently requests them, Associates suddenly respond. Margaret offers a similar example when people do not respond to requests made by her staff but do so when she gets involved. She laments, "Why would you do it because I say . . . either you can do it or you can't." Leaders may not be getting all of the information that they need to be sufficiently aware of this perceived power differential.

However, followers also demonstrate behaviors suggesting the playing field had been levelled. Kolten once received feedback from a follower that she and her peers do not feel compelled to react to a communication just because it is from a partner. Both Kolten and Farren also noted that followers do not feel shy about expressing criticisms. Farren said, "Everything gets challenged in our company."

There may also be gaps in self-awareness of one's impact. As Farren noted, "I think I sometime underestimate the power that I have." Malcolm believed that his manager is open-minded and very open to being challenged. However, he also recognized that this openness might not be readily apparent to a new follower who might perceive his manager's behavior as dominating rather than having "passion about his ideas." Malcolm said, "He's just very candid and straightforward, but sometimes I think people at first, they misinterpret that; that he doesn't want to hear their ideas or he doesn't want them to disagree with him. And nothing could be further from the truth."

One final indicator of perceived power differential resides in the question of decision authority. The majority of the leaders acknowledge their decision authority. However, their goal is to distribute that authority among their followers. The point of issue is who actually makes the final decision. Lawrence said, "I prefer not to call the decision, I prefer others to get to that decision, but I'm just saying, from a leadership point of view, you have to know when enough is enough." However, Rosemary commented that "at some point, within any organization and at any level, whoever is the decision-maker needs to be able to state the decision: 'Here is the decision and the decision needs to be followed.'"

Kolten said about decision-making in the company that most are made at the point of need, within the projects. He said that corporate decision-making is widely shared through consultation.

> The Engagement Manager will make decisions related to their project. So anything related to their project from budgets to work schedules to what not. And those are the majority of the decisions that are made in the company, and are made at the level of the Engagement Manager. Those are generally done in consultation either with their Managing Partner or with the teams, or both. The decisions of the company, the responsibility for that is done by the partners in terms of kind of like, you know, legal decisions or in terms of structural decisions or in terms of policy decisions. Often times those are done in consultation or in collaboration with one or two other folks that might have interest in that particular area where decisions are ultimately being made. The process by which these decisions are made are pretty—it's pretty consultative in the sense that everybody always has an ability to input into it regardless of where they are in the organization—has the ability to input into it.

However, as stated by Holly, there was a widely shared view that decisions made by the senior leaders could be more transparent to others. Samantha confirmed this desire when she said,

> At this point, it's in some ways very much a top-down approach even with the feedback cycles that are sometimes implemented. And, in some respects, I think

people have an interest in more democratic processes. And, not only that, but, more efficient processes because, occasionally, it ends up becoming quite a bottleneck at the partner level. [The senior leaders are] all incredibly busy and so it can be hard to get time for the quantity of decisions that they, ultimately, have to make because of the way that the company is structured. And, I think, it would be beneficial to have more distributed decision-making opportunities just to make the company run better.

At the time of the interviews the senior leaders had only just started publishing the Minutes of their weekly meetings, and this was receiving positive feedback. Again, in terms of the degree of transparency and distribution of decision-making power, the distinctions are nuanced. The senior leaders perceive that they are widely distributing decision-making authority, whereas the followers believe there is room for improvement.

Summary of Key Findings

This chapter presented the key findings concerning how 25 leaders across two organizations construct power. The findings emerged from analyses of individual interviews as data from both group interactions and documentation addressing organizational systems and structures. They were represented by six themes. The first three themes explored how leaders think about power. Of significance was their perception that power is not something that can be possessed. Rather, it is seen as a neutral social force that one develops the capacity to exercise. Leaders must make a choice in how they express power. The most common expressions are domination and mutualism. Collaborative leaders require the capacity to express both, but show a preference for mutualistic forms. The findings indicate that these leaders choose to express mutualism in terms of influencing through inspiring followers, helping to release their inherent capacities, and modeling the use of power. Participants defined the abuse of power in terms of domination over another. There were gender differences in this abuse of power. Males tended to overuse power and reflected on the need to use self-constraint. Conversely, females believed they abused their power when they underused it and did not respond in a manner necessitated by the situation.

Analysis of group observations revealed the fourth theme of relational equality that was explored from the perspective of shared ownership, participatory decision-making, respect for others, and transparency in communication. Systems and structures revealed one common theme of innovating strategic frameworks across both organizations. The findings indicated that the two organizations were principle-centered and values-driven. They considered collaboration as being central to how they function, they consciously chose a devolved leadership structure, and they placed importance on doing social good to leave the world a better place than they found it.

Indirectly related to power, but critical for its expression, the sixth theme explored how these leaders sustained their constructions of power. The findings indicated that leadership practices, character, and culture were all essential support mechanisms. Leadership practices included such actions as consulting others, participatory decision-making, working through conflict, putting others ahead of oneself, promoting relational equality, and valuing diversity. These included humility, trustworthiness, and courage. The culture they strove to create was supportive of all organizational members, both direct and indirect; it promoted continuous learning; and it felt safe for followers to fully express themselves and grow into their potential.

An important contradictory finding suggested that in spite of the efforts of these leaders, their followers continued to project power as dominance onto them. It is possible that these leaders did sometimes behave in ways that substantiated this projection. However, it is equally likely that follower projections were the result of influences from the external culture, where dominance continues to be the most common expression of power. Group observations, however limited, revealed indications of the practice of mutualistic power in both organizations.

The next chapter examines the implications of these findings, considers them in light of the scholarly literature, and draws some initial conclusions in light of the research question. Implications for scholarship and practice are considered, as are recommendations for future research.

CHAPTER FIVE

DISCUSSION

This chapter offers interpretations of the study's key findings and considers them in light of the scholarly literature. The discussion indicates where findings confirm or contest the literature and where they represent original ideas. I then present an integral model of mutualistic power based on my findings. Limitations of this study and suggestions for future research are indicated, as well as the implications of the findings for both scholarship and practice.

This study included 25 participants who were recruited from two organizations. People from within my professional network recognized the participants and their organizations for being collaborative in their approach to leadership. Data were gathered through semistructured interviews, observation of group interactions, and a review of documentation related to organizational systems and structures. These data represent both the leaders' thoughts and their actions in relation to power. Perspectives on both thought and action are needed to fully understand how a concept is being constructed. Thematic analysis was applied to all three data sources.

This study expands our understanding of collaborative leadership. The research question informing this study asks how leaders who are identified as collaborative construct power. The findings indicate that leaders who practice this approach construct power in broader terms than are generally found in the leadership literature. The leadership literature tends to consider power solely in terms of dominance. The leaders in this study demonstrate a preference for mutualistic expressions. They also create systems and structures and purposefully act to shape the organizational environment in such a way as to build and sustain their constructions.

The following discussion reviews the study results in terms of the six themes outlined in Chapter 4. The themes are reproduced in Figure 6.

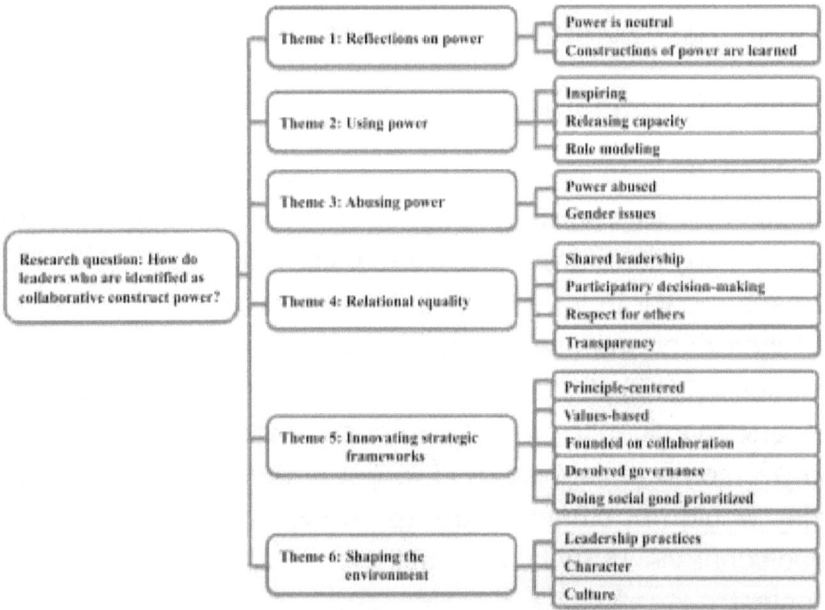

Figure 6. Research question, emergent themes, and key findings.

In several instances, discussions extend beyond the literature reviewed in Chapter 2. This has been done for two reasons. First, as previously indicated, explorations of power in the collaborative leadership literature are limited, so there are few comparable studies. Second, the intention is to demonstrate how the ideas presented here are not entirely new. They are rooted in the leadership literature of the past 100 years, suggesting that collaborative leadership is not a new idea. Instead, the findings of this study suggest that collaborative leadership represents an evolutionary step in our construction of leadership and is currently coming into focus in response to the ever-increasing complexity that characterizes our modern world. Of note is the extent to which these findings comport with the leadership theories expressed by Mary Parker Follett (Metcalf & Urwick, 1940/2013). However, they extend beyond her work. The findings in this study contribute to and promote new understandings for the scholarly discourses of both leadership and power.

Theme 1: Reflecting on Power

How the leaders in this study construct power stands in contrast to traditional treatments of power found in the leadership literature. The leadership literature tends to present power in terms of being a possession that is held by an individual and used as a form of dominance over others. Pfeffer's (1992) stance that a leader needs more power than others "to influence behavior, to change the course of events, to overcome resistance, and to get people to do things that they would not otherwise do" (p. 45) is representative of the traditional view. Such constructions are built on a footing of contest.

By contrast, the leaders in this study construct power in broader terms, including, but not limited to the traditional conceptualization of power as dominance over another. They view power as a neutral social force and believe that one needs to learn or to develop the capacity to express power.

Neutrality means that power is neither positive nor negative. The charge is determined by how it is employed. These leaders demonstrate a preference for constructing power in mutualistic terms. Mutualistic power originates with the work of Follett (Héon et al., 2014; Metcalf & Urwick, 1940/2013) and is reflective of the power discourses found in the feminist, peace, and systems literatures (Karlberg, 2005). Although overshadowed by the dominant discourse, it is also present within the leadership literature.

Expressing power in mutualistic terms means to use power-with as opposed to power-over others. Follett viewed mutualistic power to be a consensual, integrative, and transformative form that is jointly developed between leaders and followers. Increased capacity is an emergent property of both the individuals and the system. Mutualistic power can also mean power-sharing (Karlberg, 2005). Kouzes and Posner (1987/2002) believed that power sharing increases the competence, confidence, and accountability of followers and is, therefore, of benefit to individuals and the organization. Fletcher and Käufer (2003) posited that the practice of shared or fluid power dynamics is essential for shared leadership to evolve. They also suggest that engagement between leaders and followers must advance to the level of generative dialogue (Scharmer, 2000). This entails full engagement by all participants to lead the process.

Participants expressed power as being either positive or negative, where positive power is understood to represent mutualistic relations, and negative power signifies constraining relations. Fletcher (2004) raised concerns about constructing power as neutral in the absence of considerations about the implications for gender. She posited that such failure "may unwittingly undermine organizational efforts to adopt these new models and limit their transformational potential" (p. 648).

In the discussions of subsequent themes, it will be evident that the leaders in this study appear to share Fletcher's concern and have endeavored to address such concerns through their leadership practices, the character they cultivate, and the culture and environment they cocreate and make efforts to sustain. While gender is not specifically discussed, equality of all parties is.

The leaders in this study make conscious choices about how they construct power. Most indicate that they became aware of their having a choice as a direct result of a defining experience. The range of their experiences covered a wide spectrum from reflecting on personally abusing power to witnessing courageous acts by others. The ages when they had these experiences varied from early teenage years through to adulthood, suggesting that there are not temporal limitations to such learning. Having choice and learning to use power aligns with the idea that it is a socially constructed concept. That is, if power were an object that could be possessed, it would have a fixed nature rather than a mutable one that is subject to choice. Margaret, one of the participants, underlines this idea of the socially constructed nature of power when she recollects, "There's a famous quote from *Game of Thrones* . . . 'power lies where people think it lies.'"

Making a conscious choice to construct power in mutualistic terms is the first of several indications in this study that these leaders strive to balance agency and communion. Agency is associated with expressions of power as dominance, and communion represents cooperation, nurturing, and emphasizing others. Bakan (1966) coined these two terms to represent our primary behavioral motivations. Employing mutualistic power requires a sense of agency, but it also requires a willingness to share power, which is a communal motivation.

The findings of this first theme of reflecting on power comport with Karlberg's (2005) model of power. He presented power as a capacity rather than a possession, where capacity is a quality that can be learned. The capacity for power resides within each of us. While its expression can be constrained by another it cannot be taken away, whereas possessions are external to people and can be. Thus, power as capacity is a theory based on abundance and power as a possession is one informed by scarcity.

It is worthy of note that Karlberg (2005) acknowledged Mary Parker Follett's contributions to the ongoing construction of mutualistic power. It is also important to note that power-to, the third locution of power in his model, is almost absent from the data in the main study. There were so few comments that they did not warrant discussion here. Comments were more prevalent in the pilot study. This does not necessarily mean that the participants do not construct power as power-to, only that the concept was rarely mentioned.

Theme 2: Using Power

As part of the data collection interview, leaders were asked what power means to them, and to share their stories of using power. *Influencing* was the term most repeated when the participants discussed using power. However, they further explained influencing in terms of three distinct motivations: inspiring, releasing capacity, and role modeling. Influencing is frequently employed in the leadership literature in discussions of power. In fact, it is used to such an extent that it is frequently thought to be synonymous with power (Bass & Bass, 2008). Some authors indicated that both power and influence are considered to be essential for leadership. For example, Yukl's (2009) research explored how power enhances one's ability to influence and Tjosvold and Wisse (2009) commented that some scholars refer to influence as "actual or realized power" (p. 2). Together, power and influence tend to be used in the context of achieving one's purpose or agenda through others, sometimes coercively and sometimes through persuasion.

The manner in which the leaders in this study describe influencing is distinct from the wider leadership literature, with the exception of a few scholars such as Kilburg (2012). Kilburg exhorted leaders to be accountable for "influencing others in ways that consistently treat them with justice and reverence" (p. xi). The leaders in this study discuss influencing in terms of needing to persuade rather than direct, and of creating environments that draw people toward certain understandings or preferred actions. They do not discuss coercing others as an appropriate use of power.

Manipulation was a central concern to Follett (Metcalf & Urwick, 1940/2013) in her conception of leadership. There is no indication in the data that influencing is used for manipulative or self-serving purposes. Instead, these leaders view their role as one of influencing followers toward the achievement of shared goals. Decisions tend to be made collaboratively and generally represent the desire or will of the group rather than of any one individual.

Zenger, Folkman, and Edinger's (2009) research indicated followers most desire leaders who are inspiring and motivating. When the term *inspirational* is employ//ed in the leadership literature, it is generally used in the same sense as being charismatic or heroic (Bass & Bass, 2008). Such leaders are single actors who express asymmetric power (Shamir, 2012). The leaders in this study use the term *inspiring* to describe moving people toward an idea or action that serves the greater good. They use the term in the sense of accompanying others rather than viewing themselves as out ahead or in front of their followers. They prefer to employ dialogue and partnership rather than direction. This is not to suggest that collaborative leaders are incapable of being inspiring in the more traditional sense, or that they do not make visionary statements. Their preference is to inspire for purposes of drawing forth another's capacities and motivations rather than pouring in their own ideas. Follett considered the drawing forth of capacities to be fundamental to her concept of leadership (Metcalf & Urwick, 1940/2013).

Participants also underline the importance of the purpose of inspiration. They discuss it in terms of serving the greater good, and not for self-serving purposes. This idea of being focused on the greater good connects their use of power to the importance of being humble, which will be discussed as a defining personal characteristic of collaborative leaders.

The second way that these leaders use power is to release the capacity of followers. They encourage people to grow into their potential through supporting, providing resources, and removing roadblocks. The term *empowerment* is more typical of the leadership literature and tends to be defined as giving another the freedom to act independently and to make decisions and commitments on behalf of the organization (Bass & Bass, 2008; Yukl, 2013). In this sense, it represents the gifting of power from the more powerful to the less powerful (Denis et al., 2012; Fletcher & Käufer, 2003).

In this study, the term *empowerment* was used infrequently and was used primarily by only one participant. This participant was one of the youngest, newest, and most junior leaders in the study. It is possible that he had not yet fully grasped how the organization constructs power. In a second instance, a more senior leader talked about empowerment in terms of feelings that arise from within him. Instead of empowerment, these leaders spoke in terms of enabling people. For example, Samantha talked about her role as engagement manager where she understood that her role was to

> support them and guide them by sharing best practices and helping them to understand the vision of the event and to really adapt that vision as their own, integrate their own vision for their communities with the vision of [the project], and try to bring those together in a way that gets them really excited and that will, sort of, lead them through the vast amount of work it is that they have volunteered to take on in organizing this event.

Providing resources and creating environments where people can fully develop their capacities are thought to engender a sense of ownership and group unity. The idea of generating ownership and unity is not unique; it also features in discussions of empowerment (Bass & Bass, 2008). Thus, we can see that empowerment and releasing capacity are similar. What separates them is the notion of where the power originates. Empowerment suggests that power originates with the leader, whereas releasing capacity indicates that the potential for power resides within the follower. This notion of drawing forth capacities is also a cornerstone of Follet's (Metcalf & Urwick, 1940/2013) leadership theories.

Juxtaposing the two findings of inspiring and releasing capacity brings into view an important guiding principle. These leaders tend to think of followers as being full of potential that can be drawn out, rather than as empty vessels to be filled. The leader's role becomes one of supporting individuals as they develop their potential. They do this in part by offering guidance and resources, removing obstacles, and creating the conditions and environment for followers to act on their potential. This principle is also evident in Organization A's systems and structures documentation. However, it was not explicitly mentioned in the materials provided by Organization B.

The third and final term used by these leaders is *role modeling*, which they see as a form of teaching or educating. For example, several participants shared stories about how they learned from others about the use of power by observing behavior. Henry said of a personal role model that she "exercised power by walking the talk . . . she embodied a change in her and that has a tremendous pulling power." Garth stated, "I think that power sort of expresses itself in a leader maybe demonstrating a behavior and then everybody else picking up on that behavior." Samantha observed, "the fact that he shared in such an open way his concern, I thought was very powerful for all the rest of us in that it enabled us to follow suit." This notion of role modeling as a form of education comports with Karlberg's (2004) description of mutualistic power, particularly where inequalities are present. It is also evident in Follet's (Metcalf & Urwick, 1940/2013) work.

Much of our current understanding of role modeling originates in the work of Bandura (1999) in the field of social psychology. Applications of his work have found their way into the contemporary leadership literature. For example, Kouzes and Posner (1987/2002) discussed role modeling at length in their book, *The Leadership Challenge*. How the leaders in this study apply the concept comports with the leadership literature and more specifically the moral leadership literature. The findings in this study align with Brown and Trevino's (2014) study of the effects of role modeling in ethical leaders. Brown and Trevino's findings suggested that there is a moderating effect when there is proximity of followers to leaders. They found that senior leaders are too far removed from more junior leaders for learning about specific leadership behaviors to occur. Brown and Trevino's research indicated that role modeling is a "side by side" (p. 595) action that entails greater accompaniment than senior leaders are able to provide. The leaders in this study maintain proximity through minimizing hierarchy and promoting heterarchy.

Theme 3: Abusing Power

Study participants view power used to dominate another as an abuse of power, particularly when it is attached to self-serving goals. In this regard, Lawrence stated, "I think power is always used to ill effect if it's attached to ego and your own personal gain." Domination is understood to cause constraint of another. Ross said, "It's actually stopping the release of capacity." This makes sense when power is defined as being neutral. When someone uses power in a particular direction or with a charge, an imbalance is created in the system. If the direction used is domination, then those against whom the power is directed will feel constrained in some way, or diminished in their power.

This feeling of constraint is the mirror opposite of mutualistic power. Mutualistic power is intended to grow or release potential in others. Its use would tend to create a sense of balance within the system where all members would feel they have equal opportunity to express themselves. As discussed previously, inspiration, accompaniment, and releasing potential are thought to be important expressions of power. Domination represents the opposite of these expressions and manifests in behaviors ranging from being directive through to being coercive. Such behaviors can, in turn, result in a range of negative feelings on the part of those being dominated, from discontent through to fear.

How these leaders conceive of the abuse of power comports with the literature. As was noted in the literature review, power and leadership are thought to be synonymous (Bass & Bass, 2008; Burns, 1978; Gardner, 1990; Northouse, 2010; Rost, 1993; Yukl, 2013). And, as Karlberg (2005) observed, in general "power tends to be associated with competition at best, coercion or domination at worst" (p. 1). Torbert (1991) went further in stating that power is used primarily to dominate others and, as such, it is disintegrative. Follett (Metcalf & Urwick, 1940/2013) referred to power-over as being insidious. And still others commented that power is something not to be trusted (Bennis, 2003; Kanter, 1994; Pfeffer, 1992; Torbert, 1991). The participants think of power-over or power as domination in negative terms. The manner in which they juxtapose power as domination and mutualistic power is mirrored in Karlberg's model of power as capacity, where the use of power-over is understood to be adversarial, whereas power-with is thought to be integrative.

While many leaders in this study admitted to using power-over, all commented that the circumstances are rare and something they choose to avoid. This use is perhaps not unexpected, given that the participants are situated within and have been socialized by a wider culture that tends to promote power as dominance. However, when leaders self-reported using power against others they also reported feelings of discomfort. This occurred even when the outcomes were positive. For example, Kolten commented,

> When I would try to get people to do a particular thing I always tended to feel that it would deteriorate relationships. And it almost felt like you were expending something that was limited. And so you either had to be simultaneously gaining more authority and gaining more something that you were then expending by

getting people to follow that something.

Participants noted that the use of power as dominance, no matter what the justification, must be kept to a minimum. Dorothy said, "It's not something that you constantly do, because it has an ill effect on staff morale." The greatest number of cases where participants talked about using power as dominance involved taking a courageous stand for something that they strongly believed in, and that they believed would serve the greater good. An example discussed in Chapter 4 was confirming with suppliers the value of conducting social audits throughout the organization's supply chain. This notion of restraint is not well explored in the leadership literature.

Minimizing power as dominance raises a question about managing power, a central one for Tjosvold and Wisse (2009). They contended that aiming for equal power across a group is neither a realistic goal, nor in many instances a desirable one. Karlberg (2005) referred to equal power as a balance of power and noted that it can lead to stalemate. Instead of equal power, Tjosvold and Wisse suggested mutual power as an attainable goal. They define mutual power in terms of individuals having a diversity of capacities for power that become useful in varying circumstances. While the leaders in this study were neither asked about nor spoke directly to this issue, their understanding can be inferred. As will be discussed in Theme 6, these leaders value diversity. They also value different people taking the lead as appropriate where the situation warrants them to do so. Thus, it is reasonable to assume that participants would consider that they are managing power by striving to create the conditions for mutual power.

Tjosvold and Wisse (2009) also observed that involving employees in decision-making could mitigate the abuse of power. They believed it could also lessen the perception by followers of the abuse of power. This notion bears a similarity to Follet's (Metcalf & Urwick, 1940/2013) concept of integration, or finding common ground between leaders and followers. Again, the leaders in this study employ such practices. They engage in consultation and shared decision-making across levels. And they extend beyond these practices by emphasizing transparency wherever possible. While there are insufficient observational data to make the claim that the study participants never abuse their power, it is clear that they make an effort to avoid its abuse.

Gender distinctions in terms of the use of power were not intentionally explored; however, an important insight emerged with regards to the abuse of power. The findings in this study indicate that males consider their overuse of power to be abuse of power. This concept is well represented in the literature. By contrast, females believe their underutilization of power, or failure to access their internal resources to express power when needed, to be an abuse of power. With a few exceptions, the power literature rarely discusses the issue of gender power and the feminist literature does so only peripherally (Allen, 2009). As Allen pointed out, one is generally left to infer the feminist position by exploring discussions about other themes. She also noted that this discourse is "an exceptionally muddy conceptual terrain" (p. 294). Most discussions suggest that employing power as dominance is a masculine trait, while more collaborative approaches reflect feminine traits (Fletcher, 2004). However, the failure to use one's power as an abuse of power is not discussed.

A possible explanation for this perspective is that the women in this study view themselves to be equal to their male counterparts and therefore have equal capacity to manifest power in any form. Thus, when they reflect that a given situation called for them to act and they did not, they view this lack of agency as an abuse of power. It is entirely possible that the males in this study would assess themselves in the same way, but tend to focus on being agentic as a normative expectation. Allen (2009) noted that until Simone de Beauvoir published her treatise, *The Second Sex*, women were understood to represent immanence and lack of power, where men represented dominance. While contested in modern society, that perspective has not disappeared. This finding of gender and abuse of power may represent another example of how these leaders continue to be influenced by their environment despite efforts to minimize those effects.

Figure 7 offers a graphical representation of the gender distinctions in the abuse of power. Power is presented as a social force in unlimited supply. Anyone can utilize as much as they need when they need it. However, if one group accesses more than another, an imbalance may be felt across the system.

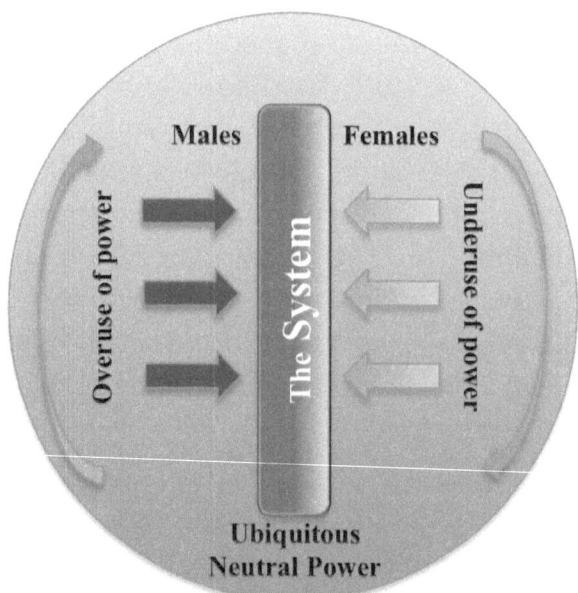

Figure 7. Gender difference in the abuse of power.

The importance of equality is a thread that weaves throughout the study findings, although it resides in the background rather than being in the foreground. More will be discussed on this topic under Theme 4. At this juncture, what is notable in the above graphic is that the achievement of equality would appear to require equal effort on the part of all parties. Males would need to rebalance their use of power or agentic behavior with more communal behavior. Conversely, females would need to rebalance their lack of agency with a greater use of power. Equality requires both genders to balance their use of agency and communality in expressing power.

Summary

The first three themes in this discussion explored how leaders construct power. The findings indicate that they view power in terms distinct from what is found in the leadership literature that addresses more traditional approaches and similar to the limited literature that explores collaborative leadership and power. Power is thought to be a ubiquitous and ample resource accessible by all. It is a neutral social force, and one learns to use it or develop the capacity to access it. These leaders think in terms of drawing out the capacity of followers to express power through such behaviors as inspiring others, releasing capacity, and role modeling. They indicate that they hold a preference for expressing power in mutualistic terms. They choose to minimize power as domination in part because of the negative impact it can have on followers, and, in part, because it stands in contradiction to the ultimate goal of relational equality. When they do use it, their intention is to serve the greater good and not promote self- concerns. While not intentionally explored, gender and power issues are in evidence. To avoid the abuse of power, males and females need to develop the capacity to express power in a balanced manner and to support one another in achieving that goal. The next three themes reinforce the study participants' construction of power and provide additional insights concerning how they build and sustain cultures that support mutualistic power.

Theme 4: Relational Equality

Analysis of observed group interactions sheds light on the relational dynamics between leaders and followers in both Organization A and B and serves to reinforce leaders' thoughts about power as described in Themes 1 through 3. The findings in this theme focus on the dynamics that result from participant interactions. Similar to the first three themes, only those findings that are common to both organizations are considered. While the data for this theme were not extensive, they did provide evidence that findings gathered from both entitative and relational perspectives complement one another and offer a broader perspective on leadership when they are juxtaposed (Uhl-Bien & Ospina, 2012). *Entitative* refers to a focus on the individual such as the data gathered through interviews, and *relational* refers to intersubjective action such as dialogue.

Denis et al. (2012) observed that at the heart of the relational perspective "leadership is fundamentally more about participation and collectively creating a sense of direction than it is about control and exercising authority" (p. 45). They explained that the perspective becomes one of *being in leadership* rather than one of *being leaders and followers*. Denis et al. described relational leadership as "a social phenomenon, as a collective process in which formally designated individuals may play a role, but from which it is impossible to ignore other actors" (p.45). Emphasis shifts from the heroic actor portrayed as the container of leadership to post- heroic leadership where the collective enacts leadership. Denis et al. also recognized that framing collaborative leadership in this manner is philosophically rooted in the work of Mary Parker Follett, and, in particular, the ideas she presented in her 1924 publication *Creative Experience*. The findings of this theme are considered first in light of her theories and then compared to the contemporary literature. In particular, the notions of democracy and relational equality are highlighted.

Individually and collectively, the four findings of shared leadership, participatory decision-making, respect for others, and transparency in communication represent and support mutualistic power. They also comport with Follett's theories of organization (Graham, 2003; Metcalf & Urwick, 1940/2013). However, it is also instructive to look back further than Follett's management writings and consider her philosophies of democracy and relational equality that subsequently informed her management writings. In *The New State*, Follett (1918) said, "We have an instinct for democracy because we have an instinct for wholeness, we get wholeness only through reciprocal relations, through infinitely expanding reciprocal relations. Democracy

is really neither extending nor including merely, but creating wholes" (p. 53). Relational equality is an essential requirement for achieving this wholeness as power differentials in consultation and decision-making would maintain distinctions and serve to constrain equal participation.

Observing participants in both of these organizations in action, there was a sense of wholeness, of collective movement, and of alignment. In Organization A, the rotation of the meeting Chair was seamless. The discussion about a topic on the agenda would end, followed by a brief pause before someone other than the originating Chair would begin to speak. For the next period of time, that person would facilitate the discussion. Following another pause, the role of Chair would shift again. Lengthy pauses were used extensively in the meeting and allowed for all voices to be heard.

In Organization B, where I was able to observe the senior leadership team in person, there was a sense of being in a space where individuals had come together to be in leadership. This was reflected in their flow of dialogue, comfort with one another, and demonstrations of mutual respect. Decision-making allowed for respectful conflict. That is, the conflict was centered on the issue and not the individuals. The agenda did not move forward until all voices were heard. Long pauses allowed time for people to consider their responses to the questions being posed. In both organizations there were clear examples of the pursuit of relational equality.

Within her philosophy of democracy, Follett (1918) promoted relational equality. She stated that

If my true self is the group-self, then my only rights are those which membership in a group gives me. The old idea of natural rights postulated the particularist individual: we know now that no such person exists. The group and the individual come into existence simultaneously. (p. 46)

This is a social constructionist or relational stance. Follett's notion of the singularity of self and group also speaks to the idea of being both agentic and communal simultaneously. Individuals need to fully bring themselves to the work of the group. There is no abandonment of self; rather, there is a heightening of self for the sake of the whole. However, individual rights and entitlements are one and the same as those of the group.

Relational equality is foundational to mutualistic power.

That is, while employees may be differentiated in terms of scope of responsibility and compensation, they are afforded the same rights in terms of relating to one another as equals and contributing to consultations. Relational equality means that everyone is afforded the same opportunity to express opinions, comment on, and make recommendations about the systems and structures of the organization.

In the contemporary leadership literature, Fletcher and Käufer (2003) discussed the unequal power relations that tend to exist in traditional systems. As a result of this differential, the powerful are attended to by the powerless without needing to ask, and the powerless must anticipate the needs of the powerful. However, when relational equality and power as releasing capacity are introduced into the system, the tension that results from unequal systemic power is resolved. The leaders in this study envision their role to be one of elevating follower capacity to express power. The goal is to attain relational equality across the system. Further reinforcement for this idea is found in Theme 6 where I discuss leader humility and the aspiration never to elevate oneself above another.

The four findings of shared leadership, participatory decision-making, respect for others, and transparency in communication are also evidenced within the relational leadership literature. Examples are found in the work of Raelin (2003) and Crevani et al. (2007). Raelin described his theory of a leaderful practice as "a model that transforms leadership from an individual property into a new paradigm that redefines leadership as a collective practice" (p. 5). His leadership framework is comprised of the four aspects of concurrent, collective, collaborative, and compassionate. Raelin's descriptions of these aspects bear a strong resemblance to this theme's four findings. Crevani et al. used the term postheroic leadership to describe relational forms of leadership. In cataloguing the primary aspects found in the literature to date, their findings also compare well with those in this theme.

The findings from the exploration of the relational dynamics between leaders and followers in both organizations comport with the theories of Follett (Metcalf & Urwick, 1940/2013) as well as with contemporary research represented here by Fletcher and Käufer (2003), Raelin (2003), and Crevani et al. (2007). The findings for Theme 4 are also complementary to how the leaders in this study describe their leadership practices discussed in Theme 6. The goal of relational equality is fundamental to mutualistic power.

Theme 5: Innovating Strategic Frameworks

Documentation relative to systems and structures provided insights into the leaders' intentions for acting on power. These documents represent artifacts of thought and action and offer evidence of how the leaders think about and intend to act on power. As Spillane and Sherer (2004) have suggested, they represent "constituting elements of human activity" (p. 7). That is, they contribute to how human activity is defined.

A single subtheme of innovating strategic frameworks emerged from the data. Strategic frameworks are defined by five aspects common to both organizations: (a) principle-centered, (b) values-based, (c) founded on collaboration, (d) devolved leadership, and (e) doing social good. As with the findings associated with how these leaders think about power, the leadership literature is replete with studies that emphasize the aspects catalogued within this theme.

The first subtheme of principle-centered leadership is a concept introduced into the leadership literature by Covey (1990/1992). He was inspired by Greenleaf's (1977/2002) theory of servant leadership. The study findings under this subtheme of principle-centered are sustainability, social justice, democracy, altruism, and profitability. These are represented as human-centered concepts that promote fairness and equity across the system. For example, one of the three pillars of sustainability is social equity, which concerns reliable prosperity for all (Bruntland & World Commission on Environment & Development, 1987). Social justice represents fairness and equality in the distribution of wealth. Democracy in decision-making means participation by all parties. Altruism represents concern for the welfare of others. Profitability addresses the need to be profitable while recognizing that it should not override social equity. The leaders in these two organizations also place a priority on doing social good, as they believe that people and organizations need to leave the planet better than they found it.

The principles of sustainability, social justice, democracy, altruism, and profitability are reflected in the leadership literature. Many are addressed in discussions of ethical and moral leadership (Northouse, 2010). However, as Rhode (2006) observed, the study of moral leadership is a subdiscipline leadership, and she referred to leadership as an "academic backwater" (p. 3). As a result, the moral leadership literature may not be visible to many leaders. However, there are growing numbers of organizations that endeavor to practice similar principles. For example, B Lab has certified over 1,000 for-profit companies in over 30 countries as B Corps—Better Corporations—that "meet rigorous standards of social and environmental performance, accountability, and transparency" (Labs, 2016). Similar initiatives to B Lab include Benefit Corporation, Bureau Veritas, and 1% for the Planet.

The second aspect of the strategic framework is values-based. Values for the leaders in the two organizations studied are also largely human-centered. They include such aspects as balance, cooperation, common good, integrity, creativity, and leadership. These or similar aspects are increasingly represented in the leadership literature (Hannah & Avolio, 2011; Kilburg, 2012; Marcic, 1997; Northouse, 2010). Thus, these are not new concepts in the leadership literature.

Another of the highest values is learning. Learning organizations, as they are discussed in the literature, are concerned with developing the capacities of employees and transforming organizations to meet changing circumstances and needs (Senge, Kleiner, Roberts, Ross, & Smith, 1994). These concepts align well with the findings of both of the organizations in this study as they both appear to be firmly committed to learning and evolving.

The third aspect of the strategic framework is collaboration. Not surprisingly, collaboration is a central concern of leaders in the two organizations in this study. Both organizations have invested significant resources to expand their learning in this area. One of the key results from their efforts includes frameworks for collaboration that can be learned and used consistently across the organization. Organization A underwrote extensive research on collaboration and invested in creating a developmental framework for all members.

Organization A leaders have committed to continuous learning about effective collaboration including holding regular reflections. Organization B worked with a consulting firm to cocreate a collaboration framework through which all future programs and projects are to be vetted. They had not developed a specific framework for leaders, but the competency of collaboration was included in their customized leadership development program. Leadership practices in both organizations were also geared to promoting collaboration across both levels and groups.

The notion of a collaborative framework is not new. One need only Google the term to find hundreds of models applicable across numerous sectors. Mendenhall and Marsh (2010) made a compelling case for integrating the theories of Mary Parker Follett and Joseph Smith with those of Joseph Raelin. While Mendenhall and Marsh's model is complementary to those developed by Organizations A and B, it is not the same. The integral model of mutualistic power emerging out of this study's findings, presented at the end of this chapter, is more comprehensive.

Devolved leadership is apparent well beyond the documentation of systems and structures. The spirit of devolution permeates almost every aspect of how these leaders approach their work. In addition to shared ownership, minimized hierarchies, and transparency in communication, devolution is apparent throughout their leadership practices. As Kellerman (2012) suggested, the study of leadership "more than anything else . . . is about the devolution of power— from those on top to those down below" (p. 3). Collaborative leadership is one rung on the ladder of evolving forms of leadership. It appears to be among the most advanced forms yet conceived of and practiced.

Doing social good is another way of saying doing altruistic deeds. The importance of this finding is not unexpected given that altruism is an important principle to these organizations. The concept of altruism appears in the literature as an aspect of spiritual, servant, and ethical leadership (Fry & Wrigglesworth, 2013; Greenleaf, 1977/2002; Northouse, 2010). Otherwise, it is not a well-discussed idea in the leadership literature. As a point of interest, in the interviews these leaders did not discuss their spiritual preferences, nor did they mention being ethical or moral, and only one leader used the term *servant leader* to describe her approach. One could surmise that they view being altruistic and doing social good as part of being an effective leader.

All of the key findings under the theme of innovating strategic frameworks are individually represented in the leadership literature, but are not combined in this manner. These strategic frameworks are more likely to be found in practice where growing numbers of organizations are building innovative strategic frameworks such as these to guide their organizations.

Theme 6: Shaping the Environment

Theme 6 explores core leadership practices, important character traits, and the aspects of culture essential for mutualistic power. Seven leadership practices were identified. Leadership practice is defined in various ways in the literature. Kouzes and Posner (1987/2002) defined leadership practices as a set of preferred behaviors that leaders employ and practice as they engage with followers. This definition is fairly typical of the leadership literature. From a relational leadership perspective, Spillane, Camburn, and Stitziel Pareja (2007) challenged the limitations of this view. They posit that interactions become an important consideration in any discussion of leadership practices.

The seven practices common to the two organizations in this study are presented in Figure 8. These practices represent a constellation of actions leaders take to shape the environment such that mutualistic power becomes a reality. However, they are largely interactive and interdependent practices. That is, they depend on the relational nature of leadership between leaders and followers. For example, consulting others and participatory decision-making require the engagement of both constituents to be enacted.

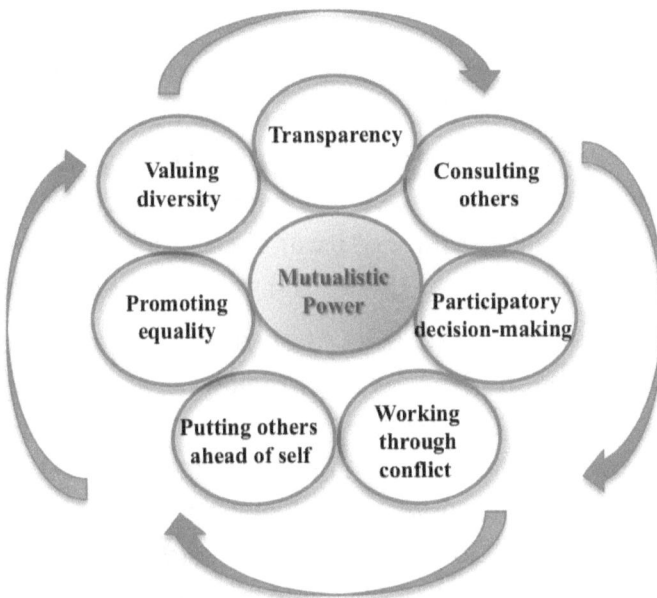

Figure 8. Constellation of leadership practices.

It is worthy of note that aspects of this theme are replicated in other data sources in this study. Similar to the strategic framework discussed in Theme 5, a desire for social justice resides at the heart of all these practices.

These seven practices are not new to the leadership literature, although they are not found in this combination, or even necessarily as leadership practices per se. For example, in the leadership literature, valuing diversity is frequently presented only as a core value or belief and not as an explicit action. Kouzes and Posner's (1987/2002) research on exemplary leadership practices, while focused on the individual or entity, introduced the notion of relational practices. In particular, they emphasized the importance of leaders engaging, inspiring, and collaborating with followers. Kouzes and Posner's fourth practice, *enable others to act,* bears a strong resemblance to the finding in this study of releasing capacity. They focused on the importance of building follower capacity, particularly as it relates to power.

The sum of these seven leadership practices is greater than their parts. Together, they serve to reinforce one another and increase their individual efficacy by functioning as a system or constellation of practices. Significantly, they enable and sustain mutualistic power. For example, participatory decision-making allows leaders to gather a diversity of perspectives.

Valuing diversity ensures that broad perspectives are brought to bear on decision-making. Transparency in communication is essential. People need to be fully informed in order to make useful contributions to consultations and decision-making. Leaders do not elevate themselves above others. They consider their higher standing within the hierarchy to represent the scope of their responsibility, not as a privilege or status. In terms of their relationship to others, leaders promote relational equality as a means to overcome power gaps. This is a core strategy, as conflict is important to effective consultation and is unlikely to emerge in the presence of power gaps. As a further means of reducing power gaps and ensuring relational equality, leaders act in a selfless manner by putting others ahead of their own needs.

The character traits these leaders value and endeavor to emulate are known elsewhere as virtues (Kilburg, 2012; Peterson & Seligman, 2004). The character traits they believe to be important are humility, trustworthiness, and courage. And discussions of virtues are most often found in the ethical and moral leadership literature (Rhode, 2006), suggesting there may be correlations between how these leaders construct power and theories of ethical and moral leadership. Humility was the most frequently mentioned virtue. It is important for these leaders to keep this in mind, as it would be easy to connect moral fortitude with self-aggrandizement. In other words, it would be easy to cross over from endeavoring to be morally strong to believing one is better than others. Not only did these leaders talk about the importance of humility, but they also represented it in the manner in which they responded to interview questions. These leaders did not appear inclined to elevate themselves in any way.

The leaders of these organizations have created positive cultures where people feel safe and motivated to learn and grow. The three findings associated with culture are a supportive culture, learning organization, and safe environment. The leaders in these organizations like their cultures. Several commented that their organization's culture is unlike others they have experienced, in a positive way. People felt genuinely supported and happy in their work. One leader explained that he left the organization, only to return. While he gained valuable experience in the years that he worked elsewhere, he wanted to return largely because of the culture. In both organizations, most of the staff has had multiple employment experiences, and so have measures of comparison.

Theme 5 introduced the idea of a learning organization as an aspect that is highly valued. Underlining this importance, learning organization appears again here in Theme 6. In this instance, it represents the idea that becoming a learning organization is a process and that patience is important for its emergence. Most of the learning is around the collaborative decision-making process. Intuitively, this makes sense, as mutualistic power and relational equality—two critical aspects of collaborative cultures—must be learned.

Edmondson (2012) identified safe environments as an important feature of collaborative cultures. The examples she used were dynamic situations that demanded the best of people. Similarly, the cultures of the organizations in this study are not stable and complacent. The work is situated on the cutting edge of change. People are challenged in their roles. Those who make a choice to work there recognize that they have found a working environment that is not easily replicated.

Additional Findings

There are three additional findings that emerge when one takes a broad perspective of the key findings previously discussed. These are the structural integration of hierarchy with heterarchy, the balancing of agency with communion, and the importance of multicultural experiences.

Hierarchy and heterarchy. Both Organizations A and B were designed around a pyramidal hierarchical structure. Organization A was headed by a group of Partners who led a number of Associates. It was a simple structure, but nonetheless hierarchical. Organization B's structure was more classical. There was a CEO at the top, supported by a senior management team whose members in turn each led a distinct functional group. However, heterarchy informs all other aspects of these organizations. Hallmark characteristics of a heterarchy are collaboration, coordination across diverse perspectives, and distributed intelligence.

Despite its hierarchical structure, Organization A's Partnership structure also reflected heterarchical intentions. For example, the single leadership team was comprised of equal yet diverse individuals. They were diverse from both a gender and a cultural perspective. There was a mixture of gender, although overbalance toward males. Culturally, the Partners were born and raised on four different continents. Each Partner had distinct responsibilities, but as a collective they coordinated the overall management and operations of the organization. Each Partner worked at some level with the

Associates, and Partners and Associates formed a unified whole at a group level.

Coordination and alignment across the group included various collaborative practices such as information dissemination, consensus building, and participative decision-making. Organizationally, the Partners regularly shared and exchanged information with Associates. Weekly Partner meeting Minutes were made available to everyone and Partners were open to comments and questions on these Minutes. Weekly organization-wide meetings were held to update everyone in the system on business priorities, and annual retreats were scheduled to enable a deeper level of reflection across the team. Issues that had a direct impact on the whole organization were consulted on with everyone, and many decisions were also made at a group level. In some cases, Associates led internal projects and in others formed subgroups with Partners to explore issues of importance. Thus, the use of heterarchical structures was extensive.

Organization B's cooperative business model lends itself to heterarchy. By its very nature it demanded more democratic leadership practices as compared to other business models such as privately held or publically traded corporations. Members owned the business and therefore had a say in how it was run. Internally, the CEO stated that he had a preference for shared governance and promoted group consensus and collective decision-making. He said that he did not want to be the final arbiter of decisions. He engaged a consulting firm to aid the senior leadership team in developing a process for effective collaboration. The senior leaders indicated that they had chosen to implement consensus building and participatory decision- making within their individual teams. Thus, the use of heterarchical structures was also extensive in Organization B.

Balancing agency and communion. The leaders in these organizations presented as being highly agentic. Their organizations were successful in no small part due to their efforts. More than one Associate commented on how hard these leaders work. From the interview data, they appeared to be both ambitious and competent. However, they also demonstrated behaviors that indicate a desire to be equally communal.

These leaders are supportive of others, promote cooperation both within their organizations and across stakeholder organizations, and are seen as acting with integrity. The organizational structures and cultures are designed around being collaborative and inclusive. As discussed above, they have designed organizations that support both hierarchical and heterarchical structures. These are clear markers of balancing agency and communality. Most importantly, in terms of balancing agency and communion, the motivation of these leaders appeared to be grounded in serving the greater good. They put others in the organization ahead of themselves and they promote altruistic behaviors on the part of all organizational members. This altruism is expressed as *doing good* in the wider environment.

From the literature, one could infer that these leaders are demonstrating enlightened self- interest, and, therefore, moral behavior (Frimer et al., 2011; Frimer et al., 2012). An expected corollary of such behavior is to choose to express mutualistic power. Choosing power as dominance indicates a preference for distance and separation and not for communal relations. These leaders choose to balance agency and communion and may well be demonstrating more advanced stages of adult development.

Multicultural experiences. One final finding of importance is the extent to which these leaders had experienced multiculturalism in their lives. Almost all of them had lived in more than one culture and, in most cases, on more than one continent. This was also an important finding of an earlier study of collaborative leaders (Davis, 2013). The precise meaning of this finding is beyond this study. However, it was sufficiently significant in two studies that it is worthy of mention. The significance may be that having experienced diversity at a personal level, these leaders sought to either create or work in structures that respect everyone and promote consensus building and decision-making.

Summary

The first three themes of reflecting on power, using power, and abusing power represent the primary ways that the leaders in this study think about power. Individually, the majority of the findings can be located within the leadership literature. As a constellation of concepts, many are found in the work of Follett (Metcalf & Urwick, 1940/2013) and Kouzes and Posner (1987/2002). These leaders frame power as a neutral force and believe that the ability to access and employ power is an inherent capacity that exists within everyone. How power is manifest is a social construction and how it is expressed is a matter of choice.

In recognizing followers as complete human beings who are full of potential, the primary ways these leaders choose to use their power is through inspiring, releasing capacity, and role modeling. They think about power in broader terms that bear a strong resemblance to Karlberg's (2005) model of power as capacity. In this model, dominance is represented in negative terms of suppression, win/lose, coercion, and oppression, and mutualistic power is expressed in positive terms of cooperation, releasing capacity, win/win, education, nurturance, and assistance. As indicated in the literature review, broader terms are necessary if the transformative potential of collaborative leadership is to be realized.

The fourth theme of relational equality emerged from the data gathered through observation of group dynamics. It is the only finding that wholly sheds light on the construction of power through action. While glimpses of action are evident in systems and structures, ultimately they represent intention or reinforcements for intentions. Relational equality is an essential outcome of mutualistic power to the extent that consensus building, decision-making, and managing through complexity are greatly enhanced when leaders and followers are engaging as relational equals.

The final two themes of innovating strategic frameworks and shaping the environment also represent leaders' actions, but are gleaned through statements of intention rather than actual, observed action. The corresponding findings shed light on how these leaders endeavor to create and sustain mutualistic power with their followers. The strategic frameworks, systems, and structures are cocreated by leaders and followers and are brought into existence through collaborative engagement.

To capture all of the findings in a composite, I borrowed from integral theory as formulated by Wilber (2011). The term integral means "comprehensive, inclusive, non- marginalizing, embracing" (Visser, 2003, p. xii). His theory integrates multiple perspectives and paradigms into one "integrated network of approaches that are mutually enriching" (p. xii). Wilber posited that every aspect of life has an interior and an exterior.

In the context of leadership, the interior signifies leader intentions, thoughts, and beliefs, as well as the cultures cocreated by leaders and their followers. Tangible aspects characterize the exterior. These include leader behaviors and actions, organizational systems and structures, and the manner in which leaders and their organizations engage with the external world.

Together, the four quadrants in integral theory provide a view of each of the distinct yet complementary perspectives of reality inclusive of the subjective, intersubjective, objective, and interobjective (Wilber, 2011). Subjective reality resides in the upper left quadrant representing intentions. Intersubjective reality is represented by the lower left quadrant representing culture. Objective reality resides in the upper right-hand quadrant representing behavior, and interobjective reality in the lower right-hand quadrant representing systems and structures. While distinct, each of the aspects within the quadrants is in a dynamic relationship to all other aspects and coevolves.

As Wilber explained, no one quadrant offers a complete picture of a phenomenon. All perspectives are needed to gain a holistic understanding. The integral model of mutualistic power shown in Figure 9 incorporates the key findings of this study. It bears repeating that almost all of the aspects that comprise this model represent original concepts. Most are well represented in the leadership literature. What is original is the gestalt the model offers in terms of leaders' thoughts and actions. When combined into a single constellation, this framework demonstrates an unprecedented view of how collaborative leaders construct mutualistic power. The model offers value for future practice and research (see Figure 9).

One final discussion concerning the data seems warranted. One of my examiners expressed concern that readers might question the data in this study. He suggested that some might perceive it to be too good to be true. Anticipating any such charge, my response is that the study participants are remarkably humble people and would be the first to point out their flaws and failings. There were hints that *shadows* were in the data, but nothing of substance. Each person's shadow or shadows seemed different from the others, apart from the one contradictory finding reviewed earlier. What I did learn is that most of these individuals had previously worked in or had known of organization environments that were entirely toxic.

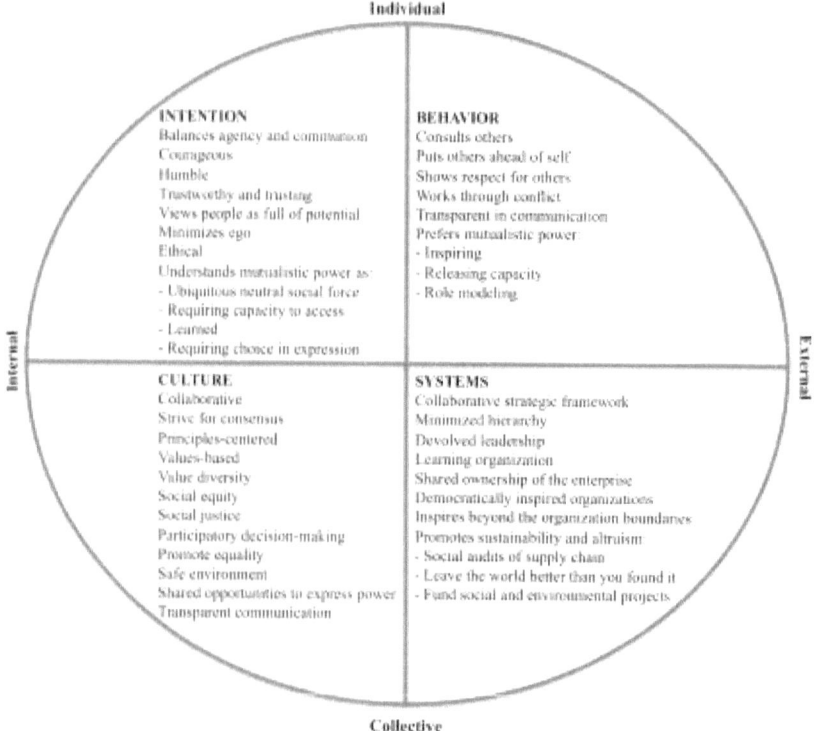

Figure 9. Integral model of mutualistic power.

From their stories of the use and abuse of power I generated two suppositions. The first supposition is that the study participants alone and together wanted to create an organization where people could thrive. In fact, Organization A documents state such a goal. Also, trust and trustworthiness was one of the highest values expressed. To engage in shadow behavior would surely undermine trust.

The second supposition is that these individuals are constructing their reality from more advanced stages of adult development than the majority of the population does (B. C. Brown, 2011). They have strived to learn new and better ways to organize in such a way that their light dims the shadow side of human behavior. I personally felt a sense of hope and possibility as I interviewed these 25 participants and worked with their data over the course of a year.

Implications for Scholarship

This study contributes to the leadership literature by integrating the discourses of collaborative leadership and power. Intuitively, one might expect leaders who practice a collaborative approach to construct power in terms other than those of dominance and coercion. How broader constructions such as mutualism manifest in this context has not previously been investigated. This study's findings indicate that when leaders choose to construct power as mutualism their choice represents more than just an alternative way to express power. It represents a different way of thinking and acting, which in turn have implications for organizational cultures, systems, and structures. These leaders recognize the tension between a preference for mutualistic power and the need to employ dominance in certain circumstances. The findings reveal that expressions of dominance are thought to be a last resort for collaborative leaders and that utilizing this approach might undermine the entire collaborative enterprise. However, the findings also indicate that there are instances where collaborative leaders do use power as dominance, but only when the intention is to serve the greater good.

Expressing mutualistic power is guided by distinct intentions and motivations. Chief among these are a motivation to balance agency with communion. Scholars have equated such intentions with moral exemplars and suggested that they are guided by enlightened self-interest (Frimer et al., 2011; Frimer et al., 2012). Based on the findings of this study, leader practice of mutualistic power is also underpinned by principles distinct from the practice of power as dominance. Democratically inspired organizational systems and structures and the promotion of relational equality are fundamental footings.

Contradictory findings suggest that followers may not fully recognize the leader's mutualistic expressions of power despite significant efforts on the part of the leader(s). For example, one participant commented on how followers might speak and act differently when leaders are present than when they are not. These findings complement a growing scholarship discussing the need for organizations to focus on developing followers.

Surprising findings reveal gender differences in how leaders perceive what constitutes their own abuse of power. Males viewed their overuse of power and females considered their underuse of power to represent abuse. However, both males and females considered the overuse of power by others to represent an abuse of power. These findings complement and extend the literature addressing gender and power. However, much of that literature focuses on power as domination and does not explore other constructions. These findings suggest that there is an issue of perceived capacity for expressing power on the part of female leaders and that power gaps may be largely self-perceived.

Finally, this study introduced the growing body of research on agency and communion to the discourses of collaborative leadership and power. Participants believe that the construction of power is learned, and that how one constructs power is ultimately a matter of choice. From the perspective of constructivist-developmental theory, a possible inference is that as adults advance in their ability to think in more complex terms, there is a greater likelihood that they will choose to construct power in mutualistic terms. Studies of influential leaders indicate that those who act with enlightened self-interest—applying their agency in service to others—tend to also be moral exemplars.

On a final note, this study also suggests that theory development lags behind practice. As indicated earlier, Google searches produce millions of hits for collaborative leadership. There are also exponentially greater numbers of organizations emerging annually whose purpose is to respond to the growing numbers of problems, challenges, and crises that characterize our modern world. Theory development is an essential cornerstone for the advancement and proliferation of innovative and creative ideas. Greater emphasis needs to be placed on leadership research that expressly addresses issues of sustainability and social justice.

Implications for Practice

This inquiry opens new vistas of understanding about collaborative leadership, particularly as it pertains to the use of power. The findings offer a useful guide to leadership and organization development practitioners. Development programs tend to focus on leader behavior from the perspective of self-awareness and on guiding culture change. Few programs address leader beliefs and character to any extent, and fewer still take the entire system into consideration. The integral model of mutualistic power offers a map of the terrain that needs to be addressed in order to build and sustain a culture that supports collaborative leadership and mutualistic power. As a starting point, exploring what it means to balance the motivations of agency and communion appears to be foundational.

Another important area of focus is follower development. The findings of this study suggest that followers may require some formal training in what it means to be a follower in a collaborative culture. It should not be assumed that followers would fully understand the outcomes that their leaders are striving to achieve without some specific and targeted development. The gap between leader intentions and follower perceptions concerning power suggests the need for, at minimum, a forum to discuss and reflect on what collaboration and mutualism mean to both parties. If the gap persists, capacity building may require a more extensive intervention. Given the importance of collaboration and the extent of the efforts on the part of leaders to create a mutualistic environment, it is surprising to find evidence that followers continue to project power as dominance onto their leaders. This suggests how challenging it can be to expunge the influences of the larger culture.

Recommendations for Future Research

This study provides insights into how leaders who are identified as collaborative construct power. This was achieved largely by conducting an exploration of this topic through an entitative lens and, to a much lesser extent, through a relational one. The entitative lens highlighted the importance leaders place on developing follower capacity. The relational lens underscored the significance of relational equality. Both aspects are fundamental to creating cultures of mutualism.

More studies are warranted to confirm and extend these findings. In particular, studies emphasizing relational dynamics would shed greater light on what Uhl-Bien and Ospina (2012) referred to as the invisible threads that connect people when they engage.

The exploration of systems and structures also provided important insights. It illuminated how these leaders confirmed and sustained their mutualistic intentions and how they extended their intentions into the wider environment. Adding a fourth perspective, leader behavior, would enable an exploration of all four quadrants of the integral model of mutualistic power. This could be achieved by interviewing followers specifically about their leaders or through the administration of surveys. Such a study would have implications for both leader development and organization development. It would provide further insights into what needs to be accentuated to create and sustain a culture that emphasizes mutualistic power.

A third recommendation is to include in future studies a measure of the stage of adult development that each of the participants has attained. Constructive-developmental theory explains the various stages of meaning making that adults may attain to. Current research suggests a positive correlation between advanced stages of development and the ability to think in more complex terms (B. C. Brown, 2011; Kegan, 1994; Sonnert & Commons, 1994; Wilber, 2011). The findings of this study suggest that the construction of mutualistic power may require the capacity to think in more complex terms. Put another way, many of the principles and practices employed by the leaders in this study indicate that they make sense of the world through the lens of more advanced worldviews. The result of such a study would have important implications for leader development (B. C. Brown, 2011; Cook-Greuter, 2004).

Limitations of the Study

There are five limitations of importance to this study. The first is sample size. While 25 participants is a reasonable number for a qualitative study (Creswell, 2013), it is still a small number and therefore limits generalization to larger populations. The second limitation is the sampling technique. Because the approach used was purposive (Neuman, 1994), meaning that I selected the organizations from within a specific population, I excluded other potential organizations not found within that population. Other organizations might have offered similar or contradictory findings. Thirdly, I did not compare and contrast the findings with organizations that do not practice collaborative leadership. However, on this last point, I did ask participants to make a comparison between these two classifications. Most participants have work experience in what could be classified as a traditional organization and they confirmed that the constructions of power by leaders in traditional organizations differ from those of collaborative organizations. In these former structures they view the use of power to be more aligned with dominance rather than mutualism.

The final limitation concerns data gathering. The contention of this study is that both thought and action are required to fully constitute a concept. To fully evaluate the construction of power by collaborative leaders entails exploring both what they think about power and what actions they take with followers. As indicated earlier, logistical challenges made direct observation difficult, particularly over a longer period of time. Observing both organizations for at least one hour offered some compensation. In the case of Organization A, the interactions of all employees were witnessed through a regularly recorded video conference call. The participants were not aware at the time of the recording that it would be shared with me. In the case of Organization B, I was able to observe the senior management team during their regular Monday morning meeting. I was able to remain in the background so that normal group dynamics might materialize. A second compensation was achieved through interviews with followers. As previously indicated, other than the six Partners of Organization A and the CEO of Organization B, the remainder of the participants are both leaders and followers. I was able to obtain perspectives on the use of power by the partners and senior leaders through these interviews.

Concluding Remarks

The purpose of this study was to explore a new leadership discourse that is emerging at the intersection of collaborative leadership and power. While collaborative leadership is a relatively new concept in the leadership literature, it has extensive antecedents. There is a long history of complementary thinking and scholarship extending back as far as ancient tribes. Mary Parker Follet, deemed a prophet of management by Peter F. Drucker (Graham, 2003), introduced concepts of collaborative leadership into the leadership lexicon almost 100 years ago. Her philosophy inspired generations of management gurus, although she was rarely acknowledged. The findings in this study are closely aligned with her theories of management.

This study explores a new discourse that is firmly rooted in the historical literature yet represents an evolutionary step in thinking about leadership. The heightening complexity that characterizes our modern world, and the concomitant problems this complexity has generated demand new ways of thinking and acting. Leadership enacted collaboratively between leaders and followers and informed by mutualistic expressions of power appears to be a much-needed response at this time in our evolutionary history. It is notable that practice appears to be outpacing scholarship. This state of affairs represents a call to action for more research into collaborative approaches to leadership.

Mary Parker Follett may have been the first to theorize mutualistic power. As a gesture of recognition and appreciation, I give her the last words in this study.

> The power of leadership is the power of integrating. This is the power which creates community.... The skillful leader then does not rely on personal force; he controls his group not by dominating but by expressing it. He stimulates what is best in us; he unifies and concentrates what we feel only gropingly and scatteringly, but he never gets away from the current of which we and he are both an integral part. He is a leader who gives form to the inchoate energy in every man. The person who influences me most is not he who does great deeds but he who makes me feel I can do great deeds. (Follett, 1918, p. 78)

References

Abele, A. E., & Wojciszke, B. (2007). Agency and communion from the perspective of self versus others. *Journal of Personality and Social Psychology, 93*(5), 751-763. doi:10.1037/0022-3514.93.5.751

Abele, A. E., & Wojciszke, B. (2013). The Big Two in social judgment and behavior. *Social Psychology, 44*, 61-62. doi:http://dx.doi.org/10.1027/1864-9335/a000137

Allen, A. (1999). *The power of feminist theory: Domination, resistance, solidarity.* Boulder, CO: Westview.

Allen, A. (2009). Gender and power. In S. R. Clegg & M. Haugaard (Eds.), *The Sage handbook of power* (pp. 293-309). Los Angeles, CA: Sage.

Arendt, H. (1969). *On violence.* San Diego, CA: Harcourt Brace Jovanovich.

B Labs, (2016). What are b corporations. Retrieved from www.bcorporation.net/what-are-b- corps

Bahá'í International Community. (1995). The prosperity of humankind. *United Nations World Summit on Social Development.* Copenhagen, Denmark.

Bakan, D. (1966). *The duality of human existence: Isolation and communion in Western man.* Boston, MA: Beacon.

Bandura, A. (1999). Social cognitive theory: An agentic perspective. *Asian Journal of Social Psychology, 2*,

21-41. doi:10.1111/1467-839X.00024

Bass, B. M., & Bass, R. (2008). *The Bass handbook of leadership: Theory, research, and managerial applications* (4th ed.). New York, NY: Free Press.

Bauer, J. J., & McAdams, D. P. (2004). Personal growth in adults' stories of life transitions. *Journal of Personality, 72*, 573-602. doi:10.1111/j.0022-3506.2004.00273.x

Bennett, N., Wise, C., Woods, P. A., & Harvey, J. (2003, Spring). Distributed leadership: A review of literature. *National College for School Leadership*, 3-57.

Bennis, W. (1999). The end of leadership: Exemplary leadership is impossible without the full inclusion, initiatives, and cooperation of followers. *Organizational Dynamics, 28*, 71-80.

Bennis, W. (2003). Thoughts on "The essentials of leadership". In P. Graham (Ed.), *Mary Parker Follett: Prophet of management* (pp. 177-181). Washington, DC: Beard Books.

Bennis, W., & Nanus, B. (2003). *Leaders: The strategies for taking charge* (2nd ed.). New York, NY: HarperCollins.

Bentz, V. M., & Shapiro, J. J. (1998). *Mindful inquiry in social research*. Thousand Oaks, CA: Sage.

Berger, P. L., & Luckmann, T. (1966/1991). *The social construction of reality: A treatise in the sociology of knowledge*. London, England: Penguin Books.

Bergman, J. Z., Rentsch, J. R., Small, E. E., Davenport, S. W., & Bergman, S. M. (2012). The shared leadership process in decision-making teams. *The Journal of*

Social Psychology, 152(1), 17-42. doi:10.1080/0022454 5.2010.538763

Bolden, R. (2011). Distributed leadership in organizations: A review of theory and research. *International Journal of Management Reviews, 13*(3), 251-269. doi:10.1111/j.1468- 2370.2011.00306.x

Bolden, R., Petrov, G., & Gosling, J. (2009). Distributed leadership in higher education: Rhetoric and reality. *Educational Management Administration & Leadership, 37*(2), 257- 277. doi:10.1177/1741143208100301

Boulding, K. E. (1990). *Three faces of power.* Newbury Park, CA: Sage.

Bradbury, H., & Lichtenstein, B. M. B. (2000). Relationality in organizational research: Exploring *The Space Between. Organization Science, 11*(5), 551-564.

Bradford, D. L., & Cohen, A. R. (1998). *Power up: Transforming organizations through shared leadership.* New York, NY: John Wiley & Sons.

Brown, B. C. (2011). *Conscious leadership for sustainability: How leaders with a late-stage action logic design and engage in sustainability initiatives.* (Doctoral dissertation). Retrieved from ProQuest Dissertations and Theses database. (UMI 3498378)

Brown, M. E., & Trevino, L. K. (2014). Do role models matter? An investigation of role modeling as an antecedent of perceived ethical leadership. *Journal of Business Ethics;* 122, 587-598. doi:10.1007/s10551-013-1769-0

Bruckmüller, S., & Abele, A. E. (2013). The density of the Big Two: How are agency and communion structurally represented? *Social Psychology, 44*, 63-74. doi:http://dx.doi.org/10.1027/1864-9335/a000145

Bruntland, G. H., & World Commission on Environment & Development, (1987). *Our common future: Report of the World Commission on Environment and Development. Oxford University.* Retrieved from http://www.un-documents.net/our-common-future.pdf

Burns, J. M. (1978). *Leadership.* New York, NY: Harper & Row.

Burrell, G., & Morgan, G. (1979). *Sociological paradigms and organisational analysis.* Surrey, England: Ashgate.

Carson, J. B., Tesluck, P. E., & Marrone, J. A. (2007). Shared leadership in teams: An investigation of antecedent conditions and performance. *Academy of Management Journal, 5*, 1217-1234. doi:10.2307/20159921

Clark, A. M. (1998). The qualitative-quantitative debate: Moving from positivism and confrontation to post-positivism and reconciliation. *Journal of Advanced Nursing, 27*, 1242-1249.

Clegg, S. R., & Haugaard, M. (2009). Discourse of power. In S. R. Clegg & M. Haugaard (Eds.), *The Sage handbook of power* (pp. 400-465). Los Angeles, CA: Sage.

Cook-Greuter, S. R. (2004). Making the case for a developmental perspective. *Industrial and Commercial Training, 36*(7), 275-281.

Corbin, J., & Strauss, A. (2008). *Basics of qualitative research* (3rd ed.). Los Angeles, CA: Sage.

Covey, S. R. (1990/1992). *Principle-centered leadership.* New York, NY: Fireside.

Creswell, J. W. (2003). *Research design: Qualitative, quantitative, and mixed methods approaches* (2nd ed.). Thousand Oaks, CA: Sage.

Creswell, J. W. (2013). *Qualitative inquiry and research design: Choosing among five approaches* (3rd ed.). Thousand Oaks, CA: Sage.

Crevani, L., Lindgren, M., & Packendorff, J. (2007). Shared leadership: A postheroic perspective on leadership as a collective construction. *International Journal of Leadership Studies, 3*, 40-67.

Crotty, M. (1998). *The foundations of social research: Meaning and perspective in the research process*. London, England: Sage.

Csikszentmihalyi, M. (1993). *The evolving self: A psychology for the third millennium*. New York, NY: HarperPerennial.

Dachler, H. P., & Hosking, D. M. (1995). The primacy of relations in socially constructing organizational realities. In D. M. Hosking, H. P. Dachler, & K. J. Gergen (Eds.), *Management and organization: Relational alternatives to individualism* (pp. 1-28). Brookfield, VT: Ashgate/Avebury. Retrieved from http://www.relational-constructionism.org/media/primacy_of_relations.pdf.

Dahl, R. A. (1957). The concept of power. *Behavioral Science, 2*(3), 201-215.

Davis, V. J. (2013). *An exploration of collaborative leadership*. Unpublished manuscript. Human Development, Fielding Graduate University, Santa Barbara, CA.

De Dreu, C. K., & Nauta, A. (2009). Self-interest and other-orientation in organizational behavior: Implications for job performance, prosocial behavior, and personal initiative. *Journal of Applied Psychology, 94*, 913-926. doi:10.1037/a0014494

Denis, J.-L., Langley, A., & Sergi, V. (2012). Leadership in the plural. *The Academy of Management Annals, 6*(1), 211-283. doi:10.1080/19416520.2012.667612

Descartes, R. (2008). *Discourse on the method of rightly conducting the reason, and seeking truth in the sciences.* Retrieved from http://www.gutenberg.org/files/59/59-h/59-h.htm

Diehl, M., Owen, S. K., & Youngblade, L. M. (2004). Agency and communion attributes in adults' spontaneous self-representations. *International Journal of Behavioral Development, 28*, 1-15. doi:10.1080/01650250344000226

Dowding, K. (2008). Power, capability and ableness: The fallacy of the vehicle fallacy. *Contemporary Political Theory, 7*, 238-258.

Drath, W. H., McCauley, C. D., Palus, C. J., Van Velsor, E., O'Connor, P. M. G., & McGuire, J. B. (2008). Direction, alignment, commitment: Toward a more integrative ontology of leadership. *The Leadership Quarterly, 19*(6), 635-653. doi:10.1016/j.leaqua.2008.09.003

Eagly, A. H., & Carli, L. L. (2007). *Through the labyrinth: The truth about how women become leaders.* Boston, MA: Harvard Business Press.

Edmondson, A. C. (2012). *Teaming: How organizations learn, innovate, and compete in the knowledge economy.* San Francisco, CA: Jossey-Bass.

Emery, F. E., & Trist, E. L. (1965). The causal texture of organizational environments. *Human Relations, 18*, 21-32.

Ensley, M. D., Hmieleski, K. M., & Pearce, C. L. (2006). The importance of vertical and shared leadership within new venture top management teams: Implications for the performance of startups. *The Leadership Quarterly, 17*(3), 217-231. doi:10.1016/j.leaqua.2006.02.002

Fairhurst, G. T., & Grant, D. (2010). The social construction of leadership: A sailing guide. *Management Communication Quarterly, 24*(2), 171-210. doi:10.1177/0893318909359697

Finch, F. E. (1977). Collaborative leadership in work settings. *The Journal of Applied Behavioral Science, 13*, 292-302. doi:10.1177/002188637701300305

Fitzsimons, D. (2012). The contribution of psychodynamic theory to relational leadership. In M. Uhl-Bien & S. M. Ospina (Eds.), *Advancing relational leadership research: A dialogue among perspectives*. Charlotte, NC: Information Age.

Fitzsimons, D., James, K. T., & Denyer, D. (2011). Alternative approaches for studying shared and distributed leadership. *International Journal of Management Reviews, 13*(3), 313-328. doi:10.1111/j.1468-2370.2011.00312.x

Fletcher, J. K. (2004). The paradox of postheroic leadership: An essay on gender, power, and transformational change. *The Leadership Quarterly, 15*, 647-661. doi:10.1016/j.leaqua.2004.07.004

Fletcher, J. K., & Käufer, K. (2003). Shared leadership: Paradox and possibility. In C. L. Pearce & J. Conger (Eds.), *Shared leadership: Reframing the hows and whys of leadership* (pp. 21-47). Thousand Oaks, CA: Sage.

Follett, M. P. (1918). *The new state – Group organization, the solution for popular government.* New York, NY: Longman, Green.

Follett, M. P. (1930). *Creative Experience.* New York, NY: Longmans, Green and Co.

Follett, M. P. (1940/2013). Power. In H. C. Metcalf & L. Urwick (Eds.), *Dynamic administration: The collected papers of Mary Parker Follett.* Mansfield Centre, CT: Martino.

Friedrich, T. L., Vessey, W. B., Schuelke, M. J., Ruark, G. A., & Mumford, M. D. (2009). A framework for understanding collective leadership: The selective utilization of leader and team expertise within networks. *The Leadership Quarterly, 20*(6), 933-958. doi:10.1016/j.leaqua.2009.09.008

Frimer, J. A., Walker, L. J., Dunlop, W. L., Lee, B. H., & Riches, A. (2011). The integration of agency and communion in moral personality: Evidence of enlightened self-interest. *Journal of Personality and Social Psychology, 101*, 149-163. doi:10.1037/a0023780

Frimer, J. A., Walker, L. J., Lee, B. H., Riches, A., & Dunlop, W. L. (2012). Hierarchical integration of agency and communion: A study of influential moral figures. *Journal of Personality, 80*, 1117-1145. doi:10.1111/j.1467-6494.2012.00764.x

Fry, L. W., & Wrigglesworth, C. G. (2013). Toward a theory

of spiritual intelligence and spiritual leadership development. *International Journal on Spirituality and Organization Leadership, 1*(1), 47-79.

Gardner, J. W. (1990). *On leadership.* New York, NY: The Free Press.

Gastil, J. (1994). A definition and illustration of democratic leadership. *Human Relations, 47*(8), 953. doi:10.1177/001872679404700805

Gergen, K. J. (1995). Relational theory and the discourses of power. In D. M. Hosking, H. P. Dachler, & K. J. Gergen (Eds.), *Management and organization: Relational alternatives to individualism* (pp. 29-50). Aldershot, England: Avebury.

Gergen, K. J. (2009). *Relational being: Beyond self and community.* New York, NY: Oxford University Press.

Gergen, M. (1995). The social construction of grievances: Constructive and constructionist approaches to a relational theory. In D. M. Hosking, H. P. Dachler, & K. J. Gergen (Eds.), Management and organization: Relational alternatives to individualism (pp. 98-103). Aldershot, England: Avebury.

Gibb, C. A. (1954/1969). Leadership. In G. Lindzey & E. Aronson (Eds.), *Handbook of social psychology* (Vol. 4, pp. 205-282). Reading, MA: Addison-Wesley.

Giddens, A. (1984). *The constitution of society: Outline of the theory of structuration.* Cambridge, England: Polity Press.

Giddens, A. (1991). Structuration theory: Past, present and future. In C. G. A. Bryant & D. Jary (Eds.), *Giddens' theory of structuration: A critical appreciation* (pp. 201-221). London, England: Routledge.

Giddens, A. (1993). *New rules of sociological method: A positive critique of interpretative sociologies.* Stanford, CA: Stanford University Press.

Gino, F. (2013). *Sidetracked: Why our decisions get derailed, and how we can stick to the plan.* Boston, MA: Harvard Business Review.

Göhler, G. (2009). 'Power to' and 'power over'. In S. R. Clegg & M. Haugaard (Eds.), *The Sage handbook of power* (pp. 27-39). London, England: Sage.

Gordon, R. (2008). *Dispersed leadership, power and change: An empirical study using a critical management framework.* Paper presented at the Australia and New Zealand Academy of Management 22nd ANZAM Conference 2008: Managing in the Pacific Century, Auckland, New Zealand. Retrieved from http://epublications.bond.edu.au/business_pubs/113/

Graham, P. (Ed.). (2003). *Mary Parker Follett: Prophet of management.* Washington, DC: Beard Books.

Gray, B. (1989). *Collaborating: Finding common ground for multiparty problems.* San Francisco, CA: Jossey-Bass.

Greenleaf, R. K. (1977/2002). *Servant leadership: A journey into the nature of legitimate power and greatness.* Mahwah, NJ: Paulist.

Greeno, J. G., Collins, A. M., & Resnick, L. B. (1996). Cognition and learning. In D. Berliner & R. Calfee (Eds.), *Handbook of Educational Psychology* (pp. 15-46). New York, NY: Macmillan.

Gronn, P. (2002). Distributed leadership. In K. Leithwood, P. Hallinger, K. Seashore-Louis, G. Furman-Brown, P. Gronn, W. Mulford, & K. Riley (Eds.), *Second international handbook of educational leadership and administration*. Dordrecht, NL: Kluwer.

Gronn, P. (2008). The future of distributed leadership. *Journal of Educational Administration, 46*(2), 141-158. doi:10.1108/09578230810863235

Gronn, P. (2009). Leadership configurations. *Leadership, 5*(3), 381-394. doi:10.1177/1742715009337770

Guba, E. G., & Lincoln, Y. S. (2005). Paradigmatic controversies, contradictions, and emerging confluences. In N. K. Denzin & Y. S. Lincoln (Eds.), *The Sage handbook of qualitative research* (3rd ed., pp. 191-216). Thousand Oaks, CA: Sage.

Guisinger, S., & Blatt, S., J. (1994). Individuality and relatedness: Evolution of a fundamental dialectic. *American Psychologist, 49*, 104-111. doi:http://psycnet.apa.org/journals/amp/

Hannah, S. T., & Avolio, B. J. (2011). Leader character, ethos, and virtue: Individual and collective considerations. *The Leadership Quarterly, 22*(5), 989-994. doi:10.1016/j.leaqua.2011.07.018

Hatcher, W. S. (1982). The concept of spirituality. *Baha'i Studies, 11*. Retrieved from http://www.bahai-studies.ca/files/BS11.Hatcher.pdf

Haugaard, M., & Clegg, S. R. (2009). Introduction: Why power is the central concept of the social sciences. In S. R. Clegg & M. Haugaard (Eds.), *The Sage handbook of power* (pp. 1-24). London, England: Sage.

Hein, G. E. (1999). Is meaning making constructivism? Is constructivism meaning making? *The Exhibitionist, 18*(2), 15-18.

Héon, F., Davis, A., Jones-Patulli, J., & Damart, S. (2014). *The essential Mary Parker Follett: Ideas we need today.* Montreal, PQ: MPF Group.

Hernandez, M., Eberly, M. B., Avolio, B. J., & Johnson, M. D. (2011). The loci and mechanisms of leadership: Exploring a more comprehensive view of leadership theory. *The Leadership Quarterly, 22*(6), 1165-1185. doi:10.1016/j.leaqua.2011.09.009

Hooker, C., & Csikszentmihalyi, M. (2003). Flow, creativity, and shared leadership. In C. L. Pearce & J. A. Conger (Eds.), *Shared leadership: Reframing the hows and whys of leadership.* Thousand Oaks, CA: Sage.

Hosking, D. M. (1995). Constructing power: Entitative and relational approaches. In D. M. Hosking, H. P. Dachler, & K. J. Gergen (Eds.), *Management and organization: Relational alternatives to individualism* (pp. 51-70). Aldershot, England: Avebury.

House, R. J., & Aditya, R. N. (1997). The social scientific study of leadership: Quo Vadis? *Journal of Management, 23*(3), 409-473.

Huang, C.-H. (2013). Shared leadership and team learning: Roles of knowledge sharing and team characteristics. *Journal of International Management Studies, 8*(1), 124-133.

Hunt, J. G., & Dodge, G. E. (2001). Leadership deja vu all over again. *Leadership Quarterly, 11*(4), 435-458.

Interpretivism. (2014). Retrieved from http://research-methodology.net/research- philosophy/interpretivism/

Jaques, E. (1990). In praise of hierarchy. *Harvard Business Review, 68*(1), 127-133.

Joiner, W. B., & Josephs, S. A. (2006). *Leadership agility: Five levels of mastery for anticipating and initiating change.* San Francisco, CA: Jossey-Bass.

Kanter, R. M. (1994). Power failure in management circuits. In L. Maineiro & C. Tromley (Eds.), *Developing managerial skills in organizational behavior: Exercises, cases, and readings* (2nd ed., pp. 322-329). Englewood Cliffs, NJ: Prentice Hall.

Karlberg, M. (2004). *Beyond the culture of contest: From adversarialism to mutualism in an age of interdependence.* Oxford, England: George Ronald.

Karlberg, M. (2005). The power of discourse and the discourse of power: Pursuing peace through discourse intervention. *International Journal of Peace Studies, 10*(1), 1-23.

Kegan, R. (1982). *The evolving self: Problems and process in human development.* Cambridge, MA: Harvard University Press.

Kegan, R. (1994). *In over our heads: The mental demands of modern life.* Cambridge, MA: Harvard University Press.

Kellerman, B. (2012). *The end of leadership.* New York, NY: HarperCollins.

Kilburg, R. R. (2012). *Virtuous leaders: Strategy, character,* and influence in the 21st century. Washington, DC: American Psychological Association.

Kouzes, J. M., & Posner, B. Z. (1987/2002). *The leadership challenge* (3rd ed.). San Francisco, CA: Jossey-Bass.

Kramer, M. W., & Crespy, D. A. (2011). Communicating collaborative leadership. *The Leadership Quarterly, 22*, 1024-1037. doi:10.1016/j.leaqua.2011.07.021

Krebs, C. (2004). *Organic constructionism and living process theory: A unified constructionist epistemology and theory of knowledge.* (Doctoral dissertation). Retrieved from ProQuest Dissertations and Theses database. (UMI No. 3184799)

Kuhn, T. S. (1962/1996). *The structure of scientific revolutions.* Chicago, IL: University of Chicago Press.

Leader effectiveness and culture: The GLOBE study. (2012). Retrieved from http://www.ccl.org/leadership/pdf/assessments/globestudy.pdf

Lewin, K., Lippitt, R., & White, R. K. (1939). Patterns of aggressive behavior in experientially created social climates. *Journal of Social Psychology, 10*(2), 271-299.

Lincoln, Y. S., & Guba, E. G. (1985). *Naturalistic Inquiry.* Newbury Park, CA: Sage Publications.

Lipman Blumen, J. (1996). *Connective leadership: Managing in a changing world.* Oxford, England: Oxford University Press.

Liu, C. C., & I Ju, C. J. (2010). Evolution of constructivism. *Contemporary Issues in Education Research, 3*(4), 63-66.

Liu, S., Hu, J., Li, Y., Wang, Z., & Lin, X. (2014). Examining the cross-level relationship between shared leadership and learning in teams: Evidence from China. *The Leadership Quarterly, 25*(2), 282-295. doi:10.1016/j.leaqua.2013.08.006

Lukes, S. (2005). *Power: A radical view* (2nd ed.). New York, NY: Palgrave Macmillan.

Manz, C. C., & Sims, H. P., Jr. (1991). SuperLeadership: Beyond the myth of heroic leadership. *Organizational Dynamics, 19*(4), 18-35.

Marcic, D. (1997). *Managing with the wisdom of love: Uncovering virtue in people and organizations.* San Francisco, CA: Jossey-Bass.

Maxwell, J. A. (2005). *Qualitative research design: An interactive approach* (2nd ed., Vol. 41). Thousand Oaks, CA: Sage.

McAdams, D. P., Hoffman, B. J., Mansfield, E. D., & Day, R. (1996). Themes of agency and communion in significant autobiographical scenes. *Journal of Personality, 64*, 339-377. doi:http://onlinelibrary.wiley.com/journal/10.1111/%28ISSN%291467-6494

Mehra, A., Smith, B. R., Dixon, A. L., & Robertson, B. (2006). Distributed leadership in teams: The network of leadership perceptions and team performance. *The Leadership Quarterly, 17*(3), 232-245. doi:10.1016/j.leaqua.2006.02.003

Mendenhall, M. E., & Marsh, W. J. (2010). Voices from the past: Mary Parker Follett and Joseph Smith on collaborative leadership. *Journal of Management Inquiry, 19*(4),

284-303. doi:10.1177/1056492610371511

Metcalf, H. C., & Urwick, L. (Eds.). (1940/2013). *Dynamic administration: The collected papers of Mary Parker Follett*. Mansfield Center, CT: Martino.

Michie, S. G., Dooley, R. S., & Fryxell, G. E. (2006). Unified diversity in top-level teams. *International Journal of Organizational Analysis, 14*(2), 130-149. doi:10.1108/10553180610742764

Morgan, G., & Smircich, L. (1980). The case for qualitative research. *Academy of Management Review, 5*(4), 491-500.

Morriss, P. (2002). *Power: A philosophical analysis*. Manchester, England: Manchester University.

Moustakas, C. (1994). *Phenomenological research methods*. Thousand Oaks, CA: Sage.

Neuman, W. L. (1994). *Socal research methods: Qualitative and quantitative approaches* (2nd ed.). Boston, MA: Allyn and Bacon.

Nisbett, R. E. (2003). *The geography of thought: How Asians and Westerners think differently . . . and why*. New York, NY: Free Press.

Noble, H., & Smith, J. (2015). Issues of validity and reliability in qualitative research. *Evidence Based Nursing, 18*(2), 34-35. doi:10.1136/eb-2015-102054

Nohria, N., & Khurana, R. (Eds.). (2010). *Handbook of leadership theory and practice: A Harvard Business School centennial colloquium*. Boston, MA: Harvard Business Press.

Northouse, P. G. (2010). *Leadership: Theory and practice* (5th ed.). Thousand Oaks, CA: Sage.

Nye, J. S., Jr. (2010). Power and leadership. In N. Nohria & R. Khurana (Eds.), *Handbook of leadership theory and practice: A Harvard Business School centennial colloquium* (pp. 305-332). Boston, MA: Harvard Business Press.

Obolensky, N. (2010). *Complex adaptive leadership: Embracing paradox and uncertainty.* Surrey, England: Grower.

Ospina, S. M., & Uhl-Bien, M. (2012). Exploring the competing bases for legitimacy. In M. Uhl- Bien & S. M. Ospina (Eds.), *Advancing relational leadership research: A dialogue among perspective.* Charlotte, NC: Information Age.

O'Toole, J., Galbraith, J., & Lawler, E. E., III. (2002). When two (or more) heads are better than one: The promise and pitfalls of shared leadership. *California Management Review, 44*(4), 65-83.

Parry, K. W., & Bryman, A. (2006). Leadership in organizations. In S. R. Clegg, C. Hardy, T. B. Lawrence, & W. R. Nord (Eds.), *The SAGE handbook of organization studies* (2nd ed., pp. 447-468). Los Angeles, CA: Sage.

Paulhus, D. L., & Trapnell, P. D. (2008). Self-presentation of personality: An agency- communion framework. In O. P. John, R. W. Robins, & L. A. Pervin (Eds.), *Handbook of personality psychology: Theory and research* (3rd ed., pp. 492-517). New York, NY: The Guilford Press.

Pearce, C. L., & Conger, J. A. (Eds.). (2003). *Shared leadership: Reframing the hows and whys of leadership.* Thousand

Oaks, CA: Sage.

Pearce, C. L., Conger, J. A., & Locke, E. A. (2008). Shared leadership theory. *The Leadership Quarterly, 19*(5), 622-628. doi:10.1016/j.leaqua.2008.07.005

Pearce, C. L., & Manz, C. C. (2005). The new silver bullets of leadership. *Organizational Dynamics, 34*(2), 130-140. doi:10.1016/j.orgdyn.2005.03.003

Pearce, C. L., Manz, C. C., & Sims, H. P., Jr. (2008). The roles of vertical and shared leadership in the enactment of executive corruption: Implications for research and practice. *The Leadership Quarterly, 19*(3), 353-359. doi:10.1016/j.leaqua.2008.03.007

Pearce, C. L., Manz, C. C., & Sims, H. P., Jr. (2009). Where do we go from here? *Organizational Dynamics, 38*(3), 234-238. doi:10.1016/j.orgdyn.2009.04.008

Pearce, C. L., & Sims, H. P., Jr. (2002). Vertical versus shared leadership as predictors of the effectiveness of change management teams: An examination of aversive, directive, transactional, transformational and empowering leader behaviors. *Group Dynamics: Theory, Research, and Practice, 6*(2), 172-197. doi:10.1037//1089-2699.6.2.172

Peterson, C., & Seligman, M. E. P. (2004). *Character strengths and virtues: A handbook and classification* (Vol. 1). Oxford, England: Oxford University Press.

Pfeffer, J. (1992). Understanding power in organizations. *California Management Review, 34*(2), 29-50.

Pfohl, S. (2008). The reality of social constructions. In J. A. Holstein & J. F. Gubrium (Eds.), *Handbook of constructionist research.* New York, NY: The Guilford Press.

Phillips, D. C., & Burbules, N. C. (2000). *Postpositivism and educational research [Kindle for Mac version].* Retrieved from Amazon.com

Pitkin, H. F. (1972). *Wittgenstein and justice: On the significance of Ludwig Wittgenstein for social and political thought.* Berkeley: University of California Press.

Podolny, J. M., Khurana, R., & Besharov, M. L. (2010). Revisiting the meaning of leadership. In N. Nohria & R. Khurana (Eds.), *Handbook of leadership theory and practice: Harvard Business School centennial colloquium* (pp. 65-106). Boston, MA: Harvard Business Press.

Rachler, F. E., & Robinson, S. (2002). Phenomenology and postpositivism: Strange bedfellows. *Western Journal of Nursing, 25,* 464-481. doi:10.1177/0193945903253909

Raelin, J. A. (2003). *Creating leaderful organizations: How to bring out leadership in everyone.* San Francisco, CA: Berrett-Koehler.

Raelin, J. A. (2006). Does action learning promote collaborative leadership? *Academy of Management Learning & Education, 5,* 152-168.

Raelin, J. A. (2011). From leadership-as-practice to leaderful practice. *Leadership, 7*(2), 195- 211. doi:10.1177/1742715010394808

Raelin, J. A. (2012). Dialogue and deliberation as expressions of democratic leadership in participatory organizational change. *Journal of Organizational Change Management, 25*(1), 7-23. doi:10.1108/09534811211199574

Rhode, D. L. (2006). *Moral leadership: The theory and practice of power, judgment, and policy.* San Francisco, CA: Jossey-Bass.

Richards, L. (2009). *Handling qualitative data: A practical guide* (2nd ed.). London, England: Sage.

Richards, L., & Morse, J. M. (2007). *Readme first for a user's guide to qualitative methods* (2nd ed.). Thousand Oaks, CA: Sage.

Rost, J. C. (1993). *Leadership for the twenty-first century.* Westport, CT: Praeger.

Rusch, E. A., Gosetti, P. P., & Mohoric, M. (1991). *The social construction of leadership: Theory to praxis.* Paper presented at the Annual Conference on Research on Women and Education, San Jose, CA. Retrieved from http://eric.ed.gov/?id=ED349662

Sangasubana, N. (2011). How to conduct ethnographic research. *The Qualitative Report, 16*(2), 567-573.

Scharmer, C. O. (2000). *Presencing: Learning from the future as it emerges.* Paper presented at the Conference On Knowledge and Innovation, Helsinki School of Economics, Finland. Retrieved from http://www.ottoscharmer.com/sites/default/files/2000_Presencing.pdf

Schein, E. H. (2012). Foreword. In A. C. Edmondson (Ed.), *Teaming: How organizations learn, innovate, and compete in the knowledge economy* (pp. xi-xiii). San Francisco, CA: Jossey-Bass.

Seers, A., Keller, T., & Wilkerson, J. M. (2003). Can team members share leadership? In C. L. Pearce & J.

Conger (Eds.), *Shared leadership: Reframing the hows and whys of leadership* (pp. 77-102). Thousand Oaks, CA: Sage.

Senge, P. M. (1990). *The fifth discipline: The art and practice of the learning organization.* New York, NY: Doubleday.

Senge, P. M., Kleiner, A., Roberts, C., Ross, R. B., & Smith, B. J. (1994). *The fifth discipline fieldbook: Strategies and tools for building a learning organization.* New York, NY: Doubleday.

Shamir, B. (2012). Leadership research or post-leadership research? Advancing leadership theory versus throwing the baby out with the bath water. In M. Uhl-Bien & S. M. Ospina (Eds.), *Advancing relational leadership research: A dialogue among perspectives* (pp. 477-500). Charlotte, NC: Information Age.

Shamir, B., & Lapidot, Y. (2003). Shared leadership in the management of group boundaries: A study of expulsions from officers' training courses. In C. L. Pearce & J. A. Conger (Eds.), *Shared leadership: Reframing the hows and whys of leadership.* Thousand Oaks, CA: Sage.

Shapiro, I. (2003). *The state of democratic theory.* Princeton, NJ: Princeton University Press.

Sivasubramaniam, N., Murry, W. D., Avolio, B. J., & Jung, D. I. (2002). A longitudinal model of effects of team leadership and group potency on group performance. *Group and Organization Management, 27,* 66-96. doi:10.1177/1059601102027001005

Sjøberg, S. (2010). Constructivism and learning. In P. Peterson, E. Baker, & B. McGaw (Eds.), *International encyclopedia of education* (3rd ed., pp. 485-490). Oxford, England: Elsevier.

Smith, T., & Karlberg, M. (2009). Articulating a consultative epistemology: Toward a reconciliation of truth and relativism. *The Journal of Bahá'í Studies, 19*(1/4), 59-99.

Social force. (n.d.). *Businessdictionary.com* Retrieved from http://www.businessdictionary.com/definition/social-force.html

Social power. (n.d.). *Businessdictionary.com* Retrieved from http://www.businessdictionary.com/definition/social-power.html

Sonnert, G., & Commons, M. L. (1994). Society and the highest stages of moral development. *Politics and the Individual, 4*(1), 31-55.

Spillane, J. P. (2005). Distributed leadership. *The Educational Forum, 69*(2), 143-150.

Spillane, J. P., Camburn, E. M., & Stitziel Pareja, A. (2007). Taking a distributed perspective to the school principal's workday. *Leadership and Policy in Schools, 6*(1), 103-125. doi:10.1080/15700760601091200

Spillane, J. P., Halverson, R., & Diamond, J. B. (2001). Investigating school leadership practice: A distributed perspective. *Educational Researcher, 30*(3), 23-28. doi:10.3102/0013189X030003023

Spillane, J. P., & Sherer, J. Z. (2004). *A distributed perspective on school leadership: Leadership practice as stretched over people and place (preliminary draft)*. Paper presented at the Annual Meeting of the American Education Association, San Diego, CA. https://www.

sesp.northwestern.edu/docs/leadstretchSPISHE.pdf

Stark, D. (2001). Heterarchy: Exploiting ambiguity and organizational diversity. *Brazilian Journal of Political Economy, 21*(1), 21-39.

Sveiby, K.-E. (2011). Collective leadership with power symmetry: Lessons from Aboriginal prehistory. *Leadership, 7*(4), 385-414.

Thorpe, R., Gold, J., & Lawler, J. (2011). Locating distributed leadership. *International Journal of Management Reviews, 13*(3), 239-250. doi:10.1111/j.1468-2370.2011.00303.x

Tjosvold, D., & Wisse, B. (2009). *Power and interdependence in organizations.* New York, NY: Cambridge University Press.

Torbert, W. R. (1991). *The power of balance: Transforming self, society, and scientific inquiry.* Newbury Park, CA: Sage.

Transformational leadership. (n.d.). *In Businessdictionary.com* Retrieved from http://www.businessdictionary.com/definition/transformational-leadership.html

Trist, E. L. (1977). Collaboration in work settings. *The Journal of Applied Behavioral Science, 13,* 268-278. doi:10.1177/002188637701300303

Uhl-Bien, M. (2006). Relational leadership theory: Exploring the social processes of leadership and organizing. *The Leadership Quarterly, 17*(6), 654-676. doi:10.1016/j.leaqua.2006.10.007

Uhl-Bien, M., Marion, R., & McKelvey, B. (2007). Complexity leadership theory: Shifting leadership from the industrial age to the knowledge era. *The Leadership Quarterly, 18*(4), 298-318. doi:10.1016/j.leaqua.2007.04.002

Uhl-Bien, M., & Ospina, S. M. (Eds.). (2012). *Advancing relational leadership research: A dialogue among perspectives*. Charlotte, NC: Information Age.

Van Maanen, J. (1979). The fact of fiction in organizational ethnography. *Administrative Science Quarterly, 24*(4), 539-550.

Van Maanen, J. (1988). *Tales of the field: On writing ethnography.* Chicago, Il: University of Chicago Press.

Van Vugt, M., Hogan, R., & Kaiser, R. B. (2008). Leadership, followership, and evolution: Some lessons from the past. *American Psychologist, 63*(3), 182-196. doi:10.1037/0003- 066X.63.3.182

Visser, F. (2003). *Ken Wilber: Thought as passion.* New York: State University of New York Press.

Vroom, V. H. (2003). Educating managers for decision making and leadership. *Management Decision, 41*(10), 968-978. doi:10.1108/00251740310509490

Wartenberg, T. E. (1990). *The forms of power: From domination to transformation*. Philadelphia, PA: Temple University Press.

Wassenaar, C. L., & Pearce, C. L. (2012). Shared leadership 2.0: A glimpse into the state of the field. In M. Uhl-Bien & S. M. Ospina (Eds.), *Advancing relational leadership research: A dialogue among perspectives* (pp. 421-432). Charlotte, NC: Information Age.

Weber, M. (1964). *The theory of social and economic*

organizations. New York, NY: The Free Press.

Wegge, J., Jeppesen, H.-J., & Weber, W. G. (2012). Broadening our perspective: We leadership is both less romantic and more democratic. *Industrial and Organizational Psychology,* 5(4), 418-420. doi:10.1111/j.1754-9434.2012.01472.x

Welzel, L., Pearce, C. L., & Hoch, J. E. (2010). Is the most effective team leadership shared? *Journal of Personnel Psychology,* 9(3), 105-116. doi:10.1027/1866-5888/a000020

Wiggins, J. S. (1991). Agency and communion as conceptual coordinates for the understanding and measurement of interpersonal behavior. In D. Cicchetti & W. M. Grove (Eds.), *Thinking clearly about psychology: Vol. 2. Personality and psychopathology* (pp. 89- 113). Minneapolis, MN: University of Minnesota Press.

Wilber, K. (2011). *A brief history of everything.* Boston, MA: Shambhala Publications. Wittgenstein, L. (1986). *Philosophical investigations* (G. E. M. Anscombe, Trans.). Oxford, England: Basil Blackwell.

Yammarino, F. J., Salas, E., Serban, A., Shirreffs, K., & Shuffler, M. L. (2012). Collectivistic leadership approaches: Putting the "We" in leadership science and practice. *Industrial and Organizational Psychology,* 5(4), 382-402. doi:10.1111/j.1754-9434.2012.01467.x

Ybarra, O., Chan, E., Park, H., Burnstein, E., Monin, B., & Stanik, C. (2008). Life's recurring challenges and the fundamental dimensions: An integration and its implications for cultural differences and similarities [Special Issue]. *European Journal of Social Psychology,*

38, 1083-1092. doi:10.1002/ejsp.559

Youngs, H. (2009). (Un)Critical times? Situating distributed leadership in the field. *Journal of Educational Administration and History, 41*(4), 377-389. doi:10.1080/00220620903211588

Yukl, G. (2009). Power and the interpersonal influence of leaders. In D. Tjosvold & B. Wisse (Eds.), *Power and interdependence in organizations*. New York, NY: Cambridge University Press.

Yukl, G. (2013). *Leadership in organizations* (8th ed.). Boston, MA: Pearson.

Zenger, J. H., Folkman, J. R., & Edinger, S. K. (2009). *The inspiring leader: Unlocking the secrets of how extraordinary leaders motivate*. New York, NY: McGraw Hill.

Footnotes

1. With this recent spurt of growth, it is not unexpected that multiple names have emerged. Some are *collective* (Friedrich et al., 2009; Yammarino et al., 2012), *complex adaptive* (Obolensky, 2010), *complexity* (Uhl-Bien et al., 2007), *connective* (Lipman Blumen, 1996), *democratic* (Gastil, 1994; Lewin et al., 1939), *dispersed* (Gordon, 2008), *distributed* (Gronn, 2008; Spillane et al., 2001), *participative* (Vroom, 2003), *post-heroic* (Bradford & Cohen, 1998; Fletcher, 2004), *relational* (Uhl-Bien & Ospina, 2012), and *shared* leadership (Crevani et al., 2007; Pearce & Conger, 2003). There are so many versions of a collaborative approach that meta-terms are being devised. Denis et al. (2012) devised the term *Leadership in the Plural* for their meta-analysis of the field.

    Collaborative leadership has also been used as the label of preference for the literaindenture that explores collaborating across boundaries (Gray, 1989).

2. Studies of collaborative leadership include have those that demonstrate its efficacy (Bergman, Rentsch, Small, Davenport, & Bergman, 2012; Carson, Tesluck, & Marrone, 2007; Mehra, Smith, Dixon, & Robertson, 2006; Pearce & Sims, 2002; Sivasubramaniam, Murry, Avolio, & Jung, 2002; Welzel, Pearce, & Hoch, 2010). Some focus on traditional leader-follower arrangements (Joiner & Josephs, 2006). Others consider teams at all levels of the organization, including top management teams (Ensley

et al., 2006; Michie, Dooley, & Fryxell, 2006; O'Toole, Galbraith, & Lawler, 2002). Hooker and Csikszentmihalyi (2003) explore group psyche and Shamir and Lapidot (2003) examine collaborative decision-making. While Hernandez et al. (2011) have suggested that shared leadership might not emerge in cultures with high power-distance orientations, recent studies indicate otherwise (Davis, 2013; Edmondson, 2012; Huang, 2013; S. Liu, Hu, Li, Wang, & Lin, 2014). More recently, studies have begun to explore collaborative leadership through relational dynamics. For example, Crevani et al. (2007) examine the collective construction of leadership.

3. This definition has been inspired by and builds on four separate definitions. The first was generated by Rost (1993) in an effort to articulate a new school of leadership. He was responding to what he saw as Burns's (1978) shortfall in achieving such a goal. The definition he chose is "Leadership is an influence relationship among leaders and followers who intend real changes that reflect their mutual purposes" (p. 102).

Pearce, Manz, and Sims (2009) build on Pearce and Conger's (2003) initial definition presented in their landmark exploration of shared leadership. Pearce et al. define shared leadership as "a dynamic, unfolding, interactive influence process among individuals, where the objective is to lead one another towards the achievement of collective goals" (p. 234). This definition bears a strong resemblance to one developed as part of the GLOBE study of leadership. Beginning in 1991, this study included 84 social scientists from 56 countries. Through their research, they agreed that leadership is "an ability to influence, motivate, and enable others to contribute to the effectiveness and success of the organizations of which they are members" (Bass & Bass, 2008, p. 23).

Finally, Drath et al. (2008) have argued that the dominant ontology of leadership composed of leaders, followers, and shared goals has less utility in a collaborative context. They posit that direction, alignment, and commitment are integrative and therefore more reflective of a collaborative. They explain that the tripod of leaders, followers, and shared goals represents the elements of leadership, whereas direction, alignment, and commitment represent the occurrence of leadership.

This definition of leadership for this study is intended to be unifying of both the entitative (elements) and relational (occurrences) perspectives, thereby combining both the aspects of collaborative leadership. Interestingly, all of these definitions are essentially rooted in a social constructionist paradigm, with the exception of the contribution from Robert House and colleagues in the GLOBE study. In that study, leadership was defined as "a person in an organization or industry who is *'exceptionally skilled at motivating, influencing, or enabling you, others, or groups to contribute to the success of the organization or task'*" (*Leader effectiveness and culture: The GLOBE study*, 2012, p. 4)

4. A Google.ca search on September 5, 2015 produced the following number of hits: Distributed leadership 6,700,000; collective leadership 6,840,000; collaborative leadership 9,600,000; relational leadership 18,800,000; shared leadership 41,200,000.

5. Collaborative institutions include hundreds of NGOs whose purpose is to respond to crises wherever they occur in the world. In the public sector, governments have

been forming economic alliances for many decades. The European Union is the most structured. While it continues to experience growing pains, it has also made significant contributions to the betterment of life for the majority of Europeans. The wealthiest nations convene at the G8 (at present, G7, with Russia's current suspension) and G20. Additionally, the United Nations has spawned a number of important institutions such as the World Bank, International Monetary Fund, the International Court of Justice, and the World Trade Organization, among others. In the private sector new forms of governance are being tested, from coCEOs, to Office of the CEO, to any number of networked and virtual structures. These forms are especially evident in entrepreneurial and high-tech organizations.

6. See http://en.wikipedia.org/wiki/List_of_corporate_collapses_and_scandals for a list of notable corporate failures that had a negative impact on the economy. Note that the annual lists become much longer starting with 2001. Company failures such as Enron, WorldCom, Tyco, and Nortel became familiar household names, and their leaders shared a similar status.

7. The reference being made is to numerous peaceful movements such as those led by Mahatma Gandhi, Martin Luther King Jr., and Nelson Mandela, and the collective movements of the Arab Spring, and the Occupy Movement that had its beginnings on Wall Street.

8. Giddens (1984, 1991, 1993) focuses on ontological concerns, challenging the recurrent dualisms such as agency/structure and subject/object prevalent in social science research. His initial motivation for developing structuration theory was in large part to rethink the

prevailing paradigm about class systems that were understood as objectified institutions (Giddens, 1991). Here objectified means that humans are subject to a class system and no amount of agency will intercede.

Giddens believes that "all claims to knowledge are in principle open to revision in the light of further information" (Giddens, 1991, p. 207). He reconstructs the ideas that uphold incommensurability across paradigms, and in so doing places humans at the center of their own existence rather than as the objects of internal and external forces that are outside of their control. He views humans as autonomous agents who have the capacity to exercise free will and structures as recursive patterns that influence or limit humans' options and impose socialization. Together, agency and structure are mutually constitutive, representing a duality whereby they are the "medium and outcome of the practices they recursively organize" (Giddens, 1984, p. 25).

Giddens (1993) believes that humans have knowing minds and take purposive action. Giddens views human actions as recursive and to some extent routinized. It is "in and through their activities agents reproduce the conditions that make these activities possible" (Giddens, 1984, p. 2). Giddens believes that the sphere of interest for the social sciences needs to be centered on social practices and their transformations (Giddens, 1991).

There are several fundamental tenants of structuration theory important to the proposed study considered here. First, agents act knowingly and have an inherent capacity to be tacitly reflexive in the moment. They are able to monitor both their own activities and those of others, as well as "monitor that monitoring" (Giddens, 1984, p. 29).

Structures are also tacitly understood. They represent a set of rules of conduct and resources that agents intentionally draw upon as "memory traces" (Giddens, 1984, p. 25) to aid in navigating through life. This duality of structure can be both constraining and enabling. Giddens notes that knowing agents have the capacity to consciously override these memory traces and devise their own social systems (Giddens, 1984, p. 25). He further defines systems as the "reproduced relations between actors or collectives, organized as regular social practices" (Giddens, 1984, p. 25).

9. Systems Mapping is a tool developed by the Systems Dynamics group at MIT largely used organizationally for process improvements and organizational transformations. Tools such as Systems Mapping make visible interrelationships, challenges, and potential solutions that would not otherwise observable. For more information, see http://mitsloan.mit.edu/group/system-dynamics/

10. Lean is a concept based on the goals of maximizing customer value while minimizing waste. For more information see the Lean Enterprise Institute at http://www.lean.org/

APPENDIX A

Introductory Letter to Potential Participants

Dear <Participant Name>,

As you know, I am a doctoral candidate at Fielding Graduate University. I am writing to ask if you would agree to be interviewed for my dissertation research.

The purpose of this research is to explore how collaborative leaders think about and use power in their role as leader. All leaders tend to use power to get things done. My interest is in learning if there is something distinct about how collaborative leaders do this. To achieve this goal, I would like to ask you questions about your background as well as your beliefs about, understanding of, and experience with power. I also want to hear stories about how you have used power in ways that aligns with your beliefs and in ways that have not.

I am also interested to learn about the organizational systems and structures that support and/or impede a leader's being collaborative in your organization. For example, I want to understand the organization structure and how it actually functions, the way that work and roles are designed and by whom, how physical spaces are laid out, how you work in a virtual space if at all, how decisions are made, and how performance evaluations and rewards support and/or discourage collaboration. I will also want to hear any additional information you believe is important for me to know to understand the power structures in your organization.

The interview should last approximately 60 to 90 minutes. In order to ensure that I capture the true essence of responses, I will be recording the interviews. All information collected will be kept confidential and participant anonymity will be maintained. Records will be retained for continued research purposes and destroyed after 5 years. Study results may be published at a later date.

If you choose to not participate I will honor your wishes without further inquiry. Please let me know if this is your decision. Should you decide to accept my invitation, I have included an **Informed Consent form that I will need you to sign and return to me**. A scanned copy is acceptable. The Informed Consent form provides answers to questions you may have, outlines potential risks and benefits of participation, and confirms confidentiality.

Upon receipt of the form I will forward a copy of the interview questions. I will send the questions ahead of our call in order that you will have some time to consider your responses. However, preparation is not required. I am offering this information for your convenience. The interview will be semistructured in that I may ask clarifying questions to gain further insights into your responses to the proposed questions.

If you agree to participate, please review the attached schedule for interviews and indicate at least two times that are convenient to you. If none of these are convenient, please suggest alternate times. And, of course, please also return a signed copy of the Informed Consent form indicating that you have read and understood it, and are in agreement. I will reply with an invitation to confirm the schedule for our call and I will forward a copy of the interview protocol.

<Participant>, thank you for your kind consideration. I look forward to your reply. In the meantime, should you have any questions I can be reached at: 905.453.1843, via email at: vjdavis@email.fielding.edu or on Skype at: vjdavisskype.

Sincerely,

Valerie J. Davis
Ph.D. Candidate

APPENDIX B

Interview Protocol

Thank you for agreeing to participate in my dissertation study. As you know, the purpose of this research is to explore how collaborative leadership from the lens of how leaders construct power.

Before we start, do you have any questions regarding the information in the Informed Consent form, your involvement in the study, or confidentiality of the information you provide? As indicated in the form, you have the option of withdrawing from the study at any time.

Do you have *any* questions before we proceed? *Answer questions.*

I will use a pseudonym to identify you. Is there one that you would prefer? If not, I can create one for you.

I will now start the recording. I will make a few introductory comments so that I am able to distinguish this interview from the others.

Opening Comments: Today's date is XXX. This is the interview for <Pseudonym>. The interview is part of a dissertation research study on collaborative leadership.

Interview Questions:

The following questions are intended to get to know a bit more about you as a person.

1. Please tell me a bit about your personal history. First, I would like to know when and where were you born and where you grew up. Please tell me about your education, work history, and any unique experiences outside of the culture in which you were raised. Were there any experiences in your childhood and/or adolescence that you believe had a large influence on your beliefs?

The next questions are intended to understand more about you in relationship to your current organization.

2. Please tell me about your current role in this organization.

   - How long have your worked here?
   - How did you come to work here?
   - What is your work history here?
   - What are you responsible for in your current role?

Exploring the organization itself.

3. Please tell me a bit about the organization.

   - How is it structured?
   - Where do you reside in the structure?
   - How are decisions made in this organization?
   - How is conflict dealt with?

Stories about the use of power.

4. As you know, this is a study about how collaborative leaders think about and use power. I am now going to ask you some questions about power.

- When you think of having power, what does that mean to you?
- How do you define power?
- Have you ever changed your thinking about what power means? If so, how has it changed? What caused you to change your thinking?
- Can you think of any particular incidents or situations that have influenced your beliefs about power?

5. Tell me a story about when you have seen power used to good effect by a leader. What made this use of power positive?

6. Can you tell me a similar story about yourself? Have you used power in this way?
   - How did you feel afterwards?
   - Why do you think you felt this way?

7. Tell me a story about when you have seen power used to ill effect either by a leader. What made this use of power negative?

8. Can you tell me a similar story about yourself? Have you used power in this way?
   - How did you feel afterwards?
   - Why do you think you felt this way?

9. (Dependent upon the responses, I may wish to ask additional questions to understand the participant's beliefs and feelings about these incidents.)

I am also interested to learn about the organizational systems and structures that support and/or impede a leader being collaborative in your organization.

10. For example, I want to understand the organization structure and how it actually functions:

   - How are work and roles designed and by whom?
   - How are physical spaces are laid out?
   - How do you work in a virtual space if at all?
   - How are decisions made?
   - How do performance evaluations and rewards support and/or discourage collaboration?
   - What is the culture here in terms of power?

I also want to hear any additional information you believe is important for me to know to understand the structures in your organization that support the use of power.

These next questions are about collaborative leadership.

11. How do you define collaborative leadership? How do you believe collaborative leadership is distinctive from other approaches to leadership?

12. What is your experience of being a collaborative leader? Can you share a story that might exemplify your experience?

13. What do you believe are the greatest advantages of being a collaborative leader?

14. What do you believe are the greatest challenges?

15. From your perspective, are there any disadvantages of being a collaborative leader?

I will conclude by asking:

1. Is there anything else that you would like to tell me that you believe would add to my understanding of

your being a collaborative leader?
2. How has this interview been for you? Is there anything you might do differently going forward based on our dialogue?

Wrap up

After reviewing the transcription of our interview I may wish to ask some clarifying questions, and you may think of things after today that you would like to add or ask. I will let you know by email whether or not this is needed.

I also want to let you know that everyone who participated in the pilot study interviews will receive a summary report of my final dissertation study.

Do you have any final questions?

Thank you again for your time and your contribution to this research project and for sharing your experience. I would like to tell you something about what I will do with this interview. I am going to analyze it along with a lot of other interviews and try to reach some more general understanding about collaborative leadership and power. Then, I will selectively make use of material from the interviews to write about what I think I have understood. So my focus will not be on writing about you or about this experience we have just shared, but about collaborative leadership and power and what sense I can make of it from what I have learned from you and other people I will have interviewed.

APPENDIX C

Organizational Documents Reviewed

Organization A:
1. Strategy: Orientation and Aspirations 2013.
2. Strategy: [Professional Membership Organization].
3. Performance Review Process.
4. Values-based capacity development framework.
5. Roles and Responsibilities
6. Employment Model and Benefits
7. Talent Management
8. Decision-making Model

Organization B:
1. 2014 Annual Report.
2. Corporate Intranet website.
3. Corporate Internet website.
4. Observations:
    a. Senior leadership team meeting
    b. Head Office layout and design.
    c. Emerging leaders luncheon with senior leaders.

APPENDIX D

Informed Consent

How leaders who are identified as collaborative construct power

You have received an invitation to participate in a research study being conducted by me, Valerie J. Davis, a doctoral student in the School of Human and Organizational Development at Fielding Graduate University, Santa Barbara, California, USA. Dr. Katrina Rogers is supervising the study. You have received an invitation to participate in this study because you use a collaborative approach to leadership.

Before you agree to participate, it is important that you read and understand the following information that describes the research study. If you have any questions after reading this form, please contact me at vjdavis@email.fielding.edu or 905.453.1843. If you do decide to volunteer to participate, please ensure sign the document on the last page of this form.

Why is this study being conducted?

Interest in and enactment of collaborative leadership appears to be increasing in multiple sectors. Current leadership literature explores collaborative leadership in the public sector, educational institutions, the nursing profession, not-for-profit organizations, and to some extent, business organizations. However, empirical studies are still limited in number. The purpose of this research is to add to the literature on this topic through the lens of power.

What is involved and how many people will take part?

This is a study for my dissertation. You qualify as a potential participant because:

1. You apply a collaborative approach to leadership.
2. You consent to participate in the study.
3. You are at least 18 years of age.

The study will consist of interviews of up to 35 people in two separate organizations. Each person's interview will last approximately 60 to 90 minutes. It will be arranged at a mutually convenient time. The interviews will be conducted through an Internet application or face-to-face whenever possible. Interviews will be recorded and subsequently transcribed so that I will be able to compare responses across all participants. At the completion of our call I will ask to schedule a brief follow-up call in the event that I have any questions resulting from a review of the interview data. The call will be cancelled if it is not required.

How will participants be selected for interviews?

Others have identified your organization as one that practices collaborative leadership. All members are requested to participate.

How long will I be in the study?

The study is being conducted in the winter of 2014/2015. It

is anticipated the interviews will be completed within that timeframe.

Will I receive study results?

A report of the study findings will be provided to the organization.

What are the risks of the study?

The risks are considered to be minimal. However, should you experience emotional discomfort during or after your participation in the interview, please let me know. I will provide you with a list of therapists in your area.

What are the benefits of taking part is this study?

You will contribute to the growing body of knowledge about collaborative leadership. In addition, you may also gain a heightened awareness about your own approach to leadership.

What about confidentiality?

The information you provide will be kept confidential. Only my supervising faculty, the transcriptionist, and I will listen to audio recordings of the interview. The Institutional Review Board (IRB) of Fielding Graduate University retains the right to access the signed Informed Consent forms and study documents.

Everyone will be covered by confidentiality agreements. The coding will be kept in a safe location accessible to me only. Identifying information will be kept separate from the interview recordings and transcripts so responses cannot be linked to participant names. Text and audio files will be stored in password-protected files.

This Informed Consent form will be destroyed approximately

five years after the study is completed. Paper files will be shredded and electronic files will be deleted.

All communications and responses will be confidential as allowed by the communication or delivery method used.

The aggregate results of this study will be discussed with my Dissertation Chair and Committee. I will most likely use quotes from participants; however, names and any identifying information will be removed and pseudonyms will be employed.

Participation is voluntary

You are free to decline to participate in the study. If you choose to participate, you may withdraw from the study at any time without negative consequences. Should you withdraw, you may request that previously provided information be removed from the study and destroyed.

The researcher is also free to terminate the study at any time.

Compensation

No compensation will be provided for participants.

Additional Information

If you have questions about any aspect of this study or your involvement, please contact me before approving this form. You may also contact the supervising faculty. The supervising faculty has provided contact information below. If you have questions or concerns about your rights as a Research Participant, contact the Fielding Graduate University IRB by email at irb@fielding.edu or by telephone at 805.898.4033.

Researcher	Dissertation Chair
Valerie J. Davis	Katrina Rogers, Ph.D.
6 Fraser Avenue Brampton, ON L6Y 1H5 Canada vjdavis@email.fielding.edu 905.453.1843	President Fielding Graduate University 2112 Santa Barbara Street Santa Barbara, CA 93105 800.340.1099
Printed name:	Date:
Signature:	

APPENDIX E

Study Participants

Order of Interview	Organization	Pseudonym	Level
	Organization A		
1		Ross	Associate
2		Dexter	Contractor
3		Nerita	Associate
4		Robert	Partner
5		Kolten	Partner
6		Nala	Associate
7		Farren	Partner
8		Holly	Associate
9		Benjamin	Partner
10		Garth	Contractor
11		Samantha	Associate
12		Henry	Partner
	Organization B		
13		Lawrence	CEO
14		Selma	Senior Leader
15		Margaret	Senior Leader
16		Rachel	Reports to Senior Leader
17		Tyrone	Senior Leader
18		Rosemary	Reports to Senior Leader

19	Dorothy	Senior Leader
20	Carl	Senior Leader
21	Frank	Senior Leader
22	Bryce	Senior Leader
23	Hannah	Two levels down from Senior Leader
24	Patricia	Reports to Senior Leader
25	Malcolm	Reports to Senior Leader

APPENDIX F

Values-based Capacity Development Framework

Organization A

Collaboration	Impact	Musing
Expression	Excellence	Outward orientation
Integration	Wisdom	Creativity
Mutualism	Stewardship	Passion
Common Good	Leadership	Learning
Fosters unity	Strategic alignment	Learning orientation
Service	Participatory	Humility
Seeks justice	Sound judgment	Self-reflection
Balance	Integrity	Discipline
Efficiency	Rectitude of conduct	Systematic
Moderation	Keeps one's word	Commitment
Centeredness	Accountability	Self-development

APPENDIX G

Governance Model Guiding Principles

Organization A

- Efficiency
- Bottom up
- Participatory/getting input in open form
- Trust
- Transparency
- Alignment with communication process
- Speed/agility
- Keep ultimate goals (strategic plans) in mind
- Gather data as much as possible to make the decision on
- Paint a picture of the desired outcome
- Explore ramifications for all involved (core team, clients, etc)
- Recognize the importance of the little things
- Have courage and be bold
- Put the decision into action (be clear, specific,

timeframes, etc)
- Regularly evaluate the outcome

(Note: Need to include democratic decision-making for the company)

APPENDIX H

Cooperative identity, values & principles

Definition

A cooperative is an autonomous association of persons united voluntarily to meet their common economic, social, and cultural needs and aspirations through a jointly-owned and democratically- controlled enterprise.

Values

Cooperatives are based on the values of self-help, self-responsibility, democracy, equality, equity and solidarity. In the tradition of their founders, cooperative members believe in the ethical values of honesty, openness, social responsibility and caring for others.

Principles

The cooperative principles are guidelines by which cooperatives put their values into practice.

1. Voluntary and Open Membership: Cooperatives are voluntary organisations, open to all persons able to use their services and willing to accept the responsibilities

of membership, without gender, social, racial, political or religious discrimination.

2. Democratic Member Control: Cooperatives are democratic organisations controlled by their members, who actively participate in setting their policies and making decisions. Men and women serving as elected representatives are accountable to the membership. In primary cooperatives members have equal voting rights (one member, one vote) and cooperatives at other levels are also organised in a democratic manner.

3. Member Economic Participation: Members contribute equitably to, and democratically control, the capital of their cooperative. At least part of that capital is usually the common property of the cooperative. Members usually receive limited compensation, if any, on capital subscribed as a condition of membership. Members allocate surpluses for any or all of the following purposes: developing their cooperative, possibly by setting up reserves, part of which at least would be indivisible; benefiting members in proportion to their transactions with the cooperative; and supporting other activities approved by the membership.

4. Autonomy and Independence: Cooperatives are autonomous, self-help organisations controlled by their members. If they enter into agreements with other organisations, including governments, or raise capital from external sources, they do so on terms that ensure democratic control by their members and maintain their cooperative autonomy.

5. Education, Training and Information: Cooperatives provide education and training for their members, elected

representatives, managers, and employees so they can contribute effectively to the development of their cooperatives. They inform the general public - particularly young people and opinion leaders - about the nature and benefits of cooperation.

6. Cooperation among Cooperatives: Cooperatives serve their members most effectively and strengthen the cooperative movement by working together through local, national, regional and international structures.

Concern for Community: Cooperatives work for the sustainable development of their communities through policies approved by their members.

For a full discussion of cooperative enterprises, see the website for the International Co-operative Alliance found at http://ica.coop/en/whats-co-op/co-operative-identity-values-principles.

APPENDIX I

Competencies of the Leadership Mastery Program

Organization B

1. Leading me: Self-awareness and authenticity.
2. Entrepreneuring: Innovative thinking and hands-on action.
3. Futuring: Conceiving what does not exist.
4. Choosing: Confident, disciplined, and courageous decision-making.
5. Empowering: It is:
    a. Unending focus on the growth of others.
    b. Motivating and inspiring others to take positive actions.
    c. Releasing control and placing trust in the capability of others.
6. Communicating: Enthusiastic, relevant, succinct, persistent, humble, and bold.
7. Executing: determination and perseverance with flexibility, collaborating and sharing resources.
8. Adapting: Quick, agile, and curious; and challenges

old idea.

9. Serving: Open door and unpretentious, aware, present, attentive, even in the midst of activity. Serving is:
   a. Collaborating gracefully and offering to clear the table.
   b. Generous with information and opportunities.
   c. Putting the organizations interest ahead of self-interest.
   d. Anticipating the needs of others.
   e. Welcoming a diversity of people and ideas.
   f. Acting in service to our members.
   g. Creating value in all things.